Making A Valedictorian

A Student, Teacher & Parent Guide to Study Skills, Better Grades & Lifelong Learning

Andrew Goliszek, Ph.D.

Mind-Body Books, Winston-Salem, NC

Cataloging-in-Publication Data

Goliszek, Andrew.
    Making a valedictorian : a student, teacher & parent guide to study
    skills, better grades & lifelong learning / Andrew Goliszek.
        p. cm.
    Includes index.
    LCCN 2012934328
    ISBN 978-0615568126

    1. Study skills.   I. Title.
  LB1049.G65 2012   371.30281

ISBN-13: 978-0615568126
ISBN-10: 0615568122

DEDICATION

To my wife, Kathy, for supporting me in whatever I do.

CONTENTS

ACKNOWLEDGMENTS

Special thanks to Erin Goliszek, one of the finest teachers I know, for her input, insight, and suggestions, and to all the dedicated educators who have made learning a joy and a priority.

Introduction

Making the decision to become the best student you can be is the most important first step in getting better grades. Having the desire to perform your best not only motivates you to learn, it makes learning easier and much more exciting. By reading this book, you're about to develop a system of learning and studying that will remain with you for the rest of your life. And as you learn the techniques that have transformed C and D students into A and B students, you'll become more and more excited about your own progress and development.

Most students in my classes are amazed at how simple it is to study, memorize, learn, and get good grades on virtually any type of exam. Once they begin to use the tricks, strategies, and techniques in this book, they easily compete with the so called "smarter" students and, in a short period of time, become so confident that they no longer worry about failure. Studying and learning actually becomes an exciting and rewarding experience.

There's really no secret to improving academic performance and becoming a top-notch student. The methods described in this book have been available in one form or another for years. Unfortunately, many students have never heard about these methods, or they learn about them when it's too late. Others stumble onto them after they graduate and realize that learning doesn't stop when school is over. The lucky ones become lifelong learners.

The chapters are arranged in a sequence that I feel makes learning much more effective. Students begin by learning the skills needed and the habits required to becoming a top student. No one is born with study skills; you learn them, either by observing others or by being taught them with the help of good teachers, especially in elementary school. If you don't develop those skills and only do what you're conditioned to do, you'll become a mediocre student because you won't believe you're capable of much more. You'll look at the A students as gifted, not realizing that in most cases the only difference is the way they study, memorize, take notes, write papers, and, in many cases, how they take tests.

As a college professor and adviser, I've seen students that I thought had great potential ruin their chances of getting jobs or getting into colleges or professional programs simply because they never learned the skills needed to get good grades. I knew these students were smarter than their grades indicated, and given the chance would have been very successful. I wrote this book so that every student can reach his or her full potential and become the person every college, graduate school, and employer is looking for.

1

Developing Study Skills

"Always do more than is required of you."
- George Patton, 1885-1945

Some students are naturals. They catch on, learn quickly, and remember facts. Others don't do as well because they have trouble paying attention or because they've never developed the kinds of study skills their successful classmates have. The difference may have nothing to do with I.Q. but with behavior and attitude, both of which have a great effect on learning and success in school.

Successful students behave in certain ways that ensure success. They're motivated, pay attention, ignore distractions that interfere with learning, and they're more relaxed. When they need help with school work, they know how to get it. None of this is inborn, but it can be learned. In my experience, most straight A students depend on hard work and self-discipline more so than on extraordinary intelligence or innate ability. In others words, they're not necessarily smarter; they simply learned how to learn.

There are four basic strategies that any student, at any level, can use to become extraordinary and get better grades. They may sound simple, but they can make a world of difference in how a student studies and performs. They are:

- Paying Attention

- Studying Effectively

- Developing Long-Term Memory

- Developing Test-Taking Skills

How to Pay Attention

For many students, the greatest challenge of the school day is just getting up in the morning, going to school, and keeping their minds from thinking about anything but the topic being discussed. The distractions students face today can be overwhelming. Unless there's a problem such as ADD, paying attention can become a habit that's easily developed and becomes stronger the more it's used. And like every other habit that's acquired over a lifetime, this one will become ingrained for life.

Habits are behavior patterns that become regular or spontaneous the more they're repeated. Over time, they become powerful conditioned responses that are incorporated into your subconscious and are triggered whenever you receive a mental cue. Like any conditioned reflex, habits are influenced by your actions, and especially by how often you do them.

Similarly, paying attention is enhanced by mental conditioning and becomes a habit as spontaneous as foot tapping or nail biting. The more you try to concentrate and pay attention, the easier it gets and the more spontaneous it will become. Eventually, listening and paying attention becomes an ingrained, spontaneous habit that is part of your normal behavior pattern.

Virtually any student can develop the habit of paying attention if he/she follows a few simple strategies. Here are four proven ways to do that:

1. **Remind yourself to focus.** Watch a sporting event and you'll notice players giving themselves a pep talk. Using words or sentences to help you focus is a good way to direct your own actions and help you pay attention. Be positive about it. For example, remind yourself to keep your eyes focused on the board while the instructor is trying to explain a topic. Make it a habit to do this and you'll be able to concentrate much better.

2. **Stop negative self-talk.** Many students talk to themselves when they're studying or listening to lectures, but the self-talk is negative. This leads to a negative attitude about school and about one's abilities. For example, don't ever say things like "it's hopeless," or "this is impossible." Instead, be positive and say, "I can do this," or "this is easy." Positive reinforcement feeds on itself and will improve your attitude and your confidence.

3. **Ask questions.** Asking questions while listening to a lecture or while studying really helps focus your attention. For example, when reading about World War II, you might ask yourself, "Which countries did Germany occupy? Which were our friends and allies? Who did Germany fight with?" As you're reading, you may also ask yourself what the paragraph was about, what the main point was, etc.

   Asking questions during a lecture doesn't need to be verbal. As the instructor is lecturing, question the things he or she is saying or writing. This is especially effective if you read the material beforehand and anticipate what the lecture will be about. Asking questions serves two purposes: it helps bring your wandering mind back to the task at hand, and it helps you remember what's being said because you become involved in the process.

4. **Set specific study goals.** Setting goals that are specific to the topic you're studying helps attention span. One goal might be to study a short lesson until you can explain the main point; another might be to solve a math problem, or to know specific names, dates, and places. Many smaller goals are much more effective in helping you stay focused than one larger goal.

A wandering mind can be overcome easily by reconditioning your brain to replace wandering with concentration. The key to reconditioning is to actively use techniques such as the ones described to force you into replacing a bad habit with a good one. Once you've done that, learning and studying will become surprisingly easy and very rewarding.

The Information Pathway

While in school, you are going to be presented with number of facts ideas, and concepts. Some of these will have to be memorized; others will need to be analyzed or just understood. The grades you make will not necessarily depend on how smart you are but rather on how well you've mastered the skills to learn those facts, ideas, and concepts.

One of the most important aspects of learning is something most students dismiss. That is, in order for new information to be remembered, it must be understood. Plowing through words on a page or memorizing facts that seem useless and unrelated is an ineffective way to learn.

Understanding a topic is not something that just happens; it takes work and requires interest in the subject and the ability to relate what's new to what you already know. This is called active learning, which is learning that requires more than just sitting back passively and allowing the teacher or the textbook to do all the work.

To develop and improve learning skills, you first have to organize material in a way that makes study effective. It doesn't matter how bad a teacher may be; it's your responsibility to get the most out of your classes through proper note-taking, efficient study habits, and good learning techniques. Just as other skills are learned through practice, the process of gathering information, organizing it, and repeating it during exams is also learned. The ideal learning process can be diagrammed in the following manner:

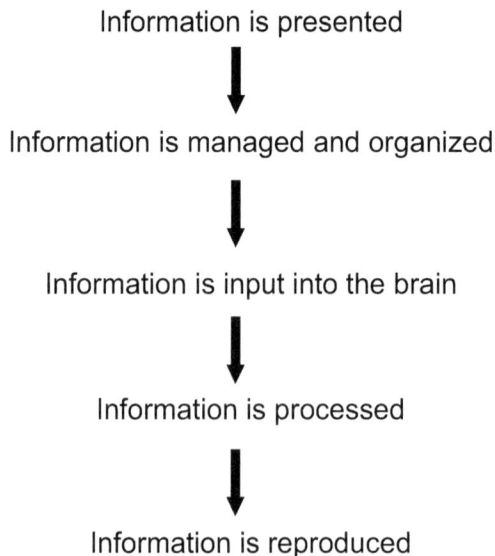

Information is presented

↓

Information is managed and organized

↓

Information is input into the brain

↓

Information is processed

↓

Information is reproduced

Information is seen and/or heard, organized through note-taking, input into the brain through reading, rewriting, and reviewing, processed through brain conditioning, and reproduced through recall. It sounds more complicated than it really is.

Effective learning involves using strategies at each stage, from listening to reading to recalling information weeks or even months later. Let's begin by looking at how you can use a simple system of gathering information, managing it in a way that makes it understandable, and then processing it in your brain so that it's there when you need it.

Learning Styles

One of the most important things you can do before you can improve your learning is to determine what kind of learner you are. Students learn in different ways. You may be a visual learner, for example, or you might learn best from either hearing or experiencing something. Therefore, you need to shape your study habits in order to perform your best. So how do you know what kind of learning style you have? The following are the most common traits for different learning styles:

Visual Learner

- Learns best by seeing rather than hearing
- Prefers diagrams, illustrations, and charts
- Likes to study alone in a quiet area
- Uses colors to highlight and outline
- Is good at spelling and math
- Likes to makes lists
- Is usually more introverted
- Likes to be shown facts rather than be told about them

Auditory Learner

- Prefers hearing lectures rather than looking at diagrams
- Likes to study in groups rather than studying alone

- Learns best when reading something aloud
- Is good at foreign languages
- Enjoys asking questions and discussing
- Is usually more extroverted
- Likes to use a tape recorder in class

Kinesthetic Learner

- Prefers doing or experiencing rather than hearing or seeing
- Enjoys labs and field trips rather than lectures
- Learns best when doing hands-on activities
- Likes to study in groups
- Participates in sports, dance, or other physical activities
- Is not good in spelling
- Can't study for long periods of time

We all learn by a combination of seeing, hearing, and doing. But by adjusting some of your study habits to fit your dominant learning style, you'll be much more successful in your classes. For example, if you're more of a visual learner, draw lots of diagrams and charts in your notes, make lists, and use colored highlighters.

If you're more of an auditory learner, that is you listen well and can absorb information better by hearing than by watching or observing, then study by reading out loud, form a study group with other students, participate in discussions, ask lots of questions, etc. And if you're a kinesthetic learner, take more lab courses, study with others so that you can lecture to them, join an intramural sports team, take a few more breaks so that you don't get burned out, etc.

The days when students were expected to study and learn only one way are long gone. Teachers realize that everyone is different and each student learns in his/her own unique way. To be the most successful student you can be, recognize what your learning style is and then change your study habits to reflect that style.

Managing Your Notes

The first step in improving learning skills is managing and organizing the information given to you. This could be difficult if the instructor isn't good at organizing his or her material to begin with. But as long as you have the organizational tools needed to overcome a poor lecture, it shouldn't really matter.

One of the most important things a student can learn is to take good notes. I've devoted an entire chapter to just that because many students go through school frustrated, having to work harder than they would otherwise because they're such poor note-takers. Taking good notes makes classes much easier and more interesting because you learn the material faster and with more comprehension. Although chapter two talks about note-taking in detail, this is a good place to discuss some general ideas on how you can use the notes you take to improve learning. Here are four ways to do that.

1. **Familiarize yourself with the lecture material beforehand.** By knowing something about the topic, you'll recognize key ideas and words when you hear them. This will help you concentrate better on what's being said rather than worrying about not understanding the material. If you can't read over the material, at least skim through it to get the main points. Most textbooks provide outlines and roadmaps at the beginning of each chapter. Using these will make note-taking easier because you'll be anticipating what's coming up in the lecture. You'll also be able to listen and write at the same time without worrying about whether you're missing important information.

2. **As soon as possible after class, rewrite your notes in a clear and organized manner.** In all my years as a teacher, I've seen few unedited notes that I would study from. Many students' notes are a jumble of disorganized sentences and missing words. This is where rewriting is important. You can fill in missing information, clear up any gaps, eliminate clutter, and add material. The physical act of reading and rewriting your notes also reinforces what you've heard and is an excellent way to learn the material while it's still fresh in your mind. Always keep the clean, edited version at home as a safeguard against loss and take your regular notebook to class.

3. **Use folders and files to organize study materials.** Besides using a notebook, develop a system for filing papers, articles, and handouts that will be available whenever you need them. A file system prevents a lot of wasted effort looking for study materials before exams and will get you in the habit of becoming more organized and efficient.

4. **Make flash cards for things like formulas, equations, dates, definitions, etc.** If there is material you need to memorize, write it down on index cards. Every few days, go through these flash cards a few times until you have the material memorized. Always change the order of the flash cards each time you study, and study them backwards and forwards in case the question is asked in a different way. For example, if one side of an index card has a word and the other side has the definition, look at the word and come up with the definition, but the next time look at the definition and come up with the word. This way you know the material either way. Teachers will often word exams differently to make sure you know the material.

As a college professor, I find that one of the biggest problems students have is poor or ineffective organizational skills. Many of these problems are solved by learning time-management strategies. In chapter 8, I'll discuss how becoming a good time manager can often make for a good student because managing your time is crucial to getting the best grades you can.

Getting Information into Your Brain

A key step in improving study and learning skills is taking the material you've organized and inputting it into your brain in the simplest and most effective way possible. Once mastered, this skill will enable you to retrieve any information you're given in class.

The fact is that 95 percent of the most important information in a textbook can be located fairly quickly because authors and publishers who know what they're doing offer roadmaps within each chapter. You'll save yourself a lot of time and energy by reading efficiently; and that's why I devoted an entire chapter to improving reading skills. Learning to pick through written material and finding the important details you need will make studying that much easier.

Studying is more than just sitting down at a desk, opening your notebook, and reading your notes. It takes planning. Students waste a lot of time and effort because they don't realize that the amount of time spent studying is not as important as the way they spend their time studying. It's like being in the gym and watching two people work out. One spends 30 minutes training effectively, building muscle and losing fat, while the other spends two hours wasting time and never getting results. Studying is the same. Even 30 minutes of effective study is better than 4 hours of poor study.

Different non-fiction content areas require different types of learning. Once you can recognize which type of learning you need to be doing, you'll be able to absorb the material into your brain much faster. For example, when studying history, concentrate on time order or sequencing. In science comparing and contrasting is very important. For both history and science, cause and effect are also critical. And for math, question and answer learning is most important. Sometimes it helps to color code flash cards, so that you know right away what you're learning. Blue index cards might be used for formulas, green for definitions, red for important dates, etc.

One of the biggest complaints I hear from students is that there's not enough time in the day to do all their work. That's nonsense. Anyone can develop effective study and learning skills and have plenty of time in their day for school work. If that weren't true, how can so many students work a full time job and still get good grades? Here are seven things you can do that will guarantee results.

1. **Find your best study time.** Because we all have unique biological clocks, we all function differently during various time of the day. Some of us are morning people, some night owls. Our individual biological clocks dictate whether we're better off studying when we first get up in the morning or whether we're better off waiting until later in the evening.

   Although you can train yourself to study at any time of the day or night, you should find when your peak energy levels are so that you can make the most of that energy for maximum learning. To find your own peak energy levels, spend a few weeks testing out how you function at different times of the day and then study accordingly.

2. **Manage your time efficiently.** Part of effective learning is time management. In my experience as a teacher for over 25 years, most students are poor time managers. To study well, you need to stick to your biological clock and establish a schedule and a study routine. Like habits, routines become ingrained and, once established, are easy to follow. If necessary, write down a daily or weekly schedule, which might include times for study, relaxation, or seeing friends. Schedules should be flexible, allowing some shifting for work, chores or other plans as long as the shifting doesn't become constant and disruptive.

3. **Never study more than an hour at a time without a break.** The average person begins to lose concentration after about an hour. A serious mistake many students make is cramming or studying too long at any one time. Instead of absorbing information, you'll actually be wasting a lot of time and effort because your brain is not capable of maintaining a high level of concentration without a break ever so often. The rule should be to take a ten or fifteen minute break every hour or so. It's also a good idea to switch subjects between learning sessions because studies have found that studying the same subject for prolonged periods of time can decrease your concentration and your ability to learn.

4. **Establish a study space.** Whether you live in a house or a one bedroom apartment, you have to set aside your own study area. It could be a desk or a kitchen table, but it must be fairly quiet and have good light. It's also important to always use the same area for studying because your brain will be conditioned to respond to a particular environment. That's why writers do their best writing when they have their own space. Ernest Hemingway would often do his writing while standing up, with his pad on top of a filing cabinet. That was his space and his brain responded to it. If you continually change where you study, your brain will never become conditioned to link your study area with study.

5. **Make your study space conducive to study.** To ensure successful learning, avoid distractions from noise, music, people, and activities. If you know that certain times will be especially noisy or active, eliminate them from your study schedule. Instead, schedule study during

periods of the day or evening you know will be most peaceful. Also, make sure that you have plenty of bright light because memory, concentration, and positive attitude are enhanced when you're exposed to light, especially natural daylight.

6. **Avoid foods that prevent learning.** If possible, don't eat a lot of simple carbohydrates, especially junk food, before or during your study sessions. While carbohydrates are a prime source of energy, simple sugars will cause a sudden insulin spike and then make you crash. The last thing you want to do is settle in for a nap in the middle of studying. Also, give up the habits that prevent your brain from reaching its full potential, and that is smoking and excessive drinking.

7. **Form a study group.** Being actively involved with other students and discussing study material will help you concentrate and absorb the material better. An added advantage is that someone in the study group will have information you may have missed or written down incorrectly. During your discussions, ask each other questions, do mock exams, and teach one another. According to studies, we learn only 10% of what we read but 70% of what we discuss and 90% of what we teach to others.

Questioning As a Study Technique

The way in which you study makes a big difference in how much you learn. Paying attention, managing and organizing class notes, and conditioning your brain to concentrate are all important. But for many students, the technique of questioning is one of the most effective ways to enhance learning. Study routines should always include questioning, either by yourself as a means of self-evaluation or by fellow students who are studying with you. Just as important, however, is to learn to ask yourself better questions; questions that lead to more and even deeper questions as well as answers.

Even before Socrates, who repeatedly asked his students questions as a way of teaching, questioning was a common learning strategy. Some questions require only factual recall without much thought or analysis; others are thought-provoking and force you to think on a deeper level. These are the types of questions that make you learn.

There's a difference between asking "When did Lincoln deliver his Gettysburg Address?" and "Why was Lincoln's Gettysburg Address an important speech?" Each question has its place, but the second one makes you analyze the speech in terms of the issues surrounding the Civil War. The second question makes you think and really enhances learning. Here are some effective strategies for using questioning as a study tool:

1. **When reading, ask yourself questions to find the main point.** For example, if you're reading about immigration patterns from different countries, ask questions about important issues such as "Why are these people immigrating? From which countries are they coming? How are their lives being changed? How is their immigration affecting the country they are immigrating to?" It's also a good strategy to ask the general question, "What's the point here?" All this questioning will help you focus on what you're reading and force you to study actively rather than passively.

2. **While studying notes or reading, jot down some exam questions.** By doing this, you'll uncover information that needs extra review and study. The physical act of writing down information in question form will help you understand concepts better and give you more confidence in your ability to pick out main topics and ideas. An added benefit is that you may see some of the questions on your next exam.

3. **Discuss material with other students.** Being actively involved by forming study groups and discussing topics forces you to concentrate on the material. This is why study sessions and study groups are so effective. Someone in the study group will always come up with a thought-provoking question or look at something in a way that no one else had thought of. Discussing makes you think; and taking advantage of the group's participation and total knowledge is a great way to absorb information.

4. **Immediately after a lecture, write down important questions about the topic and then answer them.** This technique forces you to think about what you did and didn't understand about the lecture. Here are some questions you should be asking:

What's the most important thing I learned today?

What didn't I understand about the lecture?

What can I do to help me understand the material better?

How can I explain in my own words what I learned today?

Left-Brained vs. Right-Brained Students

The most complex organ in the human body, the brain, is divided into two hemispheres. The right brain controls the left side of the body whereas the left brain controls the right side. Each second of your life, the right and left hemispheres communicate with each other and control all life functions. Although you use both sides of your brain when studying, the left hemisphere plays a greater role in math, language, and logic while the right hemisphere plays a lead role in visual tasks and creative thinking.

From the moment you're born, your nervous system is already developed and growing rapidly, and it's determined whether you're right or left brain dominant. For example, if you're a left-brained person, you're naturally more logical and analytical, preferring math and science. If you're a right-brained person, you're more intuitive and emotional, preferring music, literature, and art. Left-brained people are planners and organizers; right-brained people tend to do things on the spur of the moment. So which are you? Here's a comparison of right and left brained thinkers:

Right-brained thinker	Left-brained thinker
Uses relationships and intuition to find solutions	Uses data and analysis to solve problems
Creative and thinks abstractly	Logical and structured
Imaginative, intuitive, and strongly visual	Fact-driven, systematic, and rule-centered
Prefers art, music and literature	Enjoys working with numbers and calculations

Prefers groups that brainstorm and discuss	Prefers when individuals are assigned specific tasks
Flexible and emotional	More practical and reasonable
Good at remembering faces	Good at remembering names
Strong visual memory	Strong factual memory
Not good at planning	Plans, prioritizes, organizes

If you look at the characteristics of right versus left-brain people, you can see that the right hemisphere is our liberal arts side while the left is our analytical side. During embryonic development, we tend to become either right or left-brained individuals, but that doesn't mean we can't become more whole-brained. By doing things that force us to use both sides of our brain, we become well-rounded and able to get through courses that would otherwise frustrate us.

Typically, students discover early on what they're good at and which courses they will do well in. They gravitate toward those majors and become successful. Other students have no clue and go through school thinking they're just not smart enough to get ahead. This is probably truer for right-brained students who feel that subjects like math are what are holding them back.

So the key to becoming whole-brained is to develop your shadow side by doing things you wouldn't normally do. A right-brained person should be doing more puzzles, math problems, and analyzing things. A left-brained person should read more novels, take an art class, or work in groups. Forcing yourself to think outside the box will go a long way in helping you become a better student.

Math Tips for Right-Brained Students

As a teacher, I found that many students change their majors or are prevented from taking certain classes they want because of math. This is unfortunate because even right-brained thinkers can easily overcome their fear and their inability to do well in math.

The way you study math is different than the way you study other subjects like history or English. It requires a thought process that uses left-brained thinking. If you're a right-brained student and you need to develop your math skills, these suggestions that will guarantee better grades:

1. **Read more non-fiction books, magazines, and articles.** While novels and other fiction materials might be interesting and are always good to read, non-fiction forces you to use your left brain more. It makes you think in a different way, making you develop your analytical skills. Exercising your left hemisphere through reading non-fiction material is a good way to stretch your mental capacity. So don't limit your reading; expand it.

2. **Analyze graphs and tables when reading.** When reading magazine articles and books, don't just look at the figures and charts; analyze them. You may assume that a graph is there just to fill up space, but it's actually there to help you understand the material. Spend time thinking about and interpreting a graph's meaning and make sure you understand it. Get in the habit of looking at how axes are labeled, and then explain to yourself what the results of the graph, chart, or table are telling you.

3. **Work puzzles to exercise the brain.** Next time you're in a bookstore, pick up some puzzle books that include number games or math quizzes. Once you begin doing these, you'll soon notice that your ability to solve problems and work out calculations is greatly improved. Besides, anything that makes you think and use your brain is a good thing.

4. **Keep up with math homework.** Math is one of those subjects that build on previous materials and concepts. Just about everything you learn in math is based on topics you've had previously in other math courses or in previous chapters. College Algebra is based on high school Algebra, for example, Calculus is based on Algebra and Trigonometry, etc. And because math courses have specific formulas, rules, and definitions that expand in scope as the semester goes on, it's one of the easiest subjects to fall behind in. It's especially important to review previous material whenever new material is introduced so that you can reinforce what you've already learned.

Never skip a homework assignment and never go on to a new topic until you completely understand and are able to do the assigned work. Also, try to do homework as soon after class as possible, when the material is still fresh in your mind. After a few math problems, put your notes aside and try to work problems on your own without referring to any other materials. Bring the ones you can't solve to class or to your instructor's office and make sure you get them explained to you.

5. **Understand the principles.** You can often get good grades in other classes like English, History, or Foreign Language just by memorizing facts or words. This is not true in math, where it's important to know not only what a formula is but how to use it to solve a problem. This is where a lot of students run into difficulties, especially when they have to come up with solutions to word problems. They might know the formulas perfectly but have no clue how to use them. If you're having trouble with a problem, find an easier but similar one and try that. If you can solve the simpler problem, go back and retry the more difficult one.

6. **Use other math books for practice.** Besides using your own textbook, try solving problems from other textbooks. What often happens is that students get used to seeing problems written by an individual author in a certain style. When a professor then uses another source to make up exam questions, it presents a problem. By exposing yourself to different math examples, you'll become more confident in your ability to solve any problem regardless of how it's written. So for better exam success, as well as better math understanding, add some diversity to your learning.

7. **Do extra problems.** The best math students are those who spend a lot of time working homework problems because most people, especially those who are right-brained and who aren't math-oriented, need to work harder at math than any other class. In math, practicing solving problems is the key to success and good grades. Doing extra math problems not only gives you confidence in your ability to do math, it exercises the left side of your brain, which then makes you a more whole-brained student.

How to Think Critically

Critical thinking is the process of gathering material and then evaluating and analyzing it in a disciplined way. Good critical thinkers, rather than just getting and retaining information, ask lots of questions in order to understand the material, are open-minded, and use evidence, reason, and honesty to come to reasonable conclusions. In order to develop good critical thinking skills, students need to go beyond just memorizing; they need to think about what they are memorizing and why they need to memorize the information.

If you're not a critical thinker, you can learn to think critically by starting to ask yourself *why* about whatever you're reading or studying. That's because critical thinking is about questioning; and asking why is the simplest form of questioning. Think of it as an exercise that you need to do on a regular basis so that it becomes second nature. The more you do it, the more subconscious it becomes. You also need to develop certain character traits. Here are the main characteristics necessary to become a classic critical thinker:

- **Be reasonable.** Don't rely on feelings, hunches, educated guesses, and emotions; demand hard evidence, and then follow that evidence to a reasoned conclusion no matter where it might lead. Get out of the habit of needing to get quick answers, and instead use facts and reasoned arguments to solve problems.

- **Be skeptical.** By nature, critical thinkers are suspicious, inquisitive, and skeptical. They ask probing questions, which often lead to more questions, and they demand that answers are based on analysis and fact. They also challenge existing facts and beliefs and they investigate what they read in order to come to reasoned conclusions. This will be valuable no matter what career you choose, but especially if you're going into a scientific field.

- **Be curious.** Don't depend on a single source for information because this can bias your opinion. It's like watching the same news program or reading the same magazine without getting an opposing viewpoint. If you look at various sources of information, you won't be as slanted in your thinking and you'll be better prepared to make a decision based on fact rather than prejudice or opinion.

- **Be honest.** Everyone has biases and a point of view. This can get in the way of critical thinking because we tend to ignore what we don't like. Thinking critically requires brutal honesty without assumptions or prejudices.

- **Be open-minded.** Consider all possibilities and viewpoints, regardless of what you might think of them or have heard in the past. This is especially true if a viewpoint is unpopular or has been rejected before. Look for novel explanations, and always be open to alternative or different perspectives.

- **Be disciplined.** Avoid quick decisions. Critical thinkers are accurate, clear, precise, comprehensive, and thoughtful. They never make judgments based on what they feel is correct, and they never look for answers based on self-interest and personal preferences. So don't make snap decisions or go by what your gut tells you.

- **Be an effective communicator.** Analyzing information and solving complex problems is more effective when others are involved in the process of figuring out solutions. Forming a group and brain-storming is a great way to share ideas and come up with creative solutions.

- **Be curious.** Don't depend on a single source for information because this can bias your opinion. It's like watching the same news program or reading the same magazine without getting an opposing viewpoint. If you look at various sources of information, you won't be as slanted in your thinking and you'll be better prepared to make a decision based on fact rather than prejudice or opinion.

- **Be inquisitive and reflective.** Critical thinkers are naturally inquisitive because they want to know why as much as what, where, and how. Think of yourself as a trial lawyer who needs to get to the facts as well as search for the motive behind the crime. To instill curiosity, complete statements such as:

Some of the real-world applications are . . .

The key issues involved in this topic are . . .

The main question I have with this topic is . . .

The problem I have with this issue is . . .

Another way to look at this is . . .

What I'm most curious about is . . .

What I find most difficult to understand about this topic is . . .

The reason this can't be right is . . .

Questions like these lead to curiosity and future thinking. At first, you may have to force yourself to do this. Most of us just listen to a lecture or read something and not give it another thought. But once you get in the habit of being inquisitive and reflecting on the material, it becomes second nature. So to become a critical thinker, be open-minded, be skeptical and, above all, be inquisitive.

Solving Problems by Thinking Critically

Using critical thinking skills is one of the most effective ways to analyze and solve problems. That's because you'll have a clear roadmap that will guide you every step of the way until you reach a conclusion. You can break any problem down and come up with a solution by using the following 4-step approach.

1. **Identify.** The first step in solving any problem, no matter what subject, is to put it into words as clearly as possible and identify what it is that you're trying to solve. Unless you can define the problem and state what your goals are for solving it, the rest of the steps will be difficult if not impossible.

2. **Analyze.** Once you've identified what the problem is, learn more about it by researching, reading, and asking others for their perspectives and input. This is the time to drop your biases and be open-minded to fresh ideas and possibilities.

3. **Reflect.** Based on your analysis, consider a number of possibilities. Now is the time to be imaginative and creative, not closed-minded. Evaluate the effects of each solution, and consider alternatives, even if they seem at odds with current thinking. Sometimes it helps if you talk through the possibilities out loud or brainstorm with others. It also helps to free your mind of the problem and allow your subconscious to process it for a while before thinking about it again.

4. **Decide.** After identifying and analyzing the problem, and considering a number of possible solutions, choose the one that you think will work best in solving the problem.

As an alternative to traditional classroom learning, PBL is a method of critical thinking in which you actively explore issues and work with content in order to solve a problem. You can break PBL down to 6 simple steps as follows:

1. **List the important parts of the problem.** Discuss with your group the issues and the significant parts of the problem. Also discuss your current knowledge about the problem and how you can use that knowledge to help you solve it. Use each group member's strengths and expertise to assign tasks.

2. **Write the problem out in your own words.** This is a good way to get a handle on what you really need to do to solve the problem. Make sure the group agrees on the statement, and don't be afraid to change it as you get new information and input.

3. **List the possible solutions.** Brainstorm with the group and come up with a list of solutions in order from the strongest to the weakest. Don't ignore strange solutions, but concentrate on the strongest possibility.

4. **List the actions to be taken.** Make a timeline of what actions are to be taken. You may ask, "What do we need to know?" or "What do we need to do to solve the problem?"

5. **Research the knowledge and data base.** Do a literature search, read books and articles, and search data bases for information that will help you solve the problem. Assign specific tasks to members of the group so that everyone is participating.

6. **Write up the solution and defend your conclusions.** State the problem you are addressing and the conclusion, and give supporting evidence to defend that conclusion. If you are going to present your findings, you need to include: the problem statement, the data gathered and generated in the process, the analysis of the data, a summary of the process you used, the problems you ran into during the process, and the solutions and recommendations.

How Anyone Can Become a Genius

Dr. Diola Bagayoku, a Professor of Physics at Southern University has shown mathematically that just like athletes increase their performance through training and practice, students can do exactly the same thing with their study. According to Dr. Bagayoku, *"Genius is mostly the result of sustained, competitive practice."* His studies have shown that academic proficiently is directly related to adequate practice. In other words, practice makes perfect in everything you do, including learning.

The Power Law of Human Performance, as he calls it, states that the time it takes an individual to perform a task decreases as the number of times the individual practices that task increases. In other words, if students want to become geniuses, they need to train like Olympic athletes. They must have high expectations and they have to give a one hundred percent effort to their study. Practice does make perfect, both in sports and in the classroom. So regardless of race, sex, or age, every student can achieve academic excellence. As the hundreds of students that Dr. Bagayoku has trained can attest to, anyone can be made a genius.

Another way to become a genius is to become creative and imaginative. Albert Einstein used creativity, imagination, and curiosity in a way that few people before or since have. Here are some interesting quotes from a man who was the critical thinker of his time:

"The important thing is not to stop questioning. Curiosity has its own reason for existing."

"Anyone who has never made a mistake has never tried anything new."

"We can't solve problems by using the same kind of thinking we used when we created them."

The strategies and techniques I've described in this chapter are very effective once put into practice and used consistently. Over the years, I've seen average students who worked hard and learned how to study outperform even the most talented students because they were willing to put in the effort. If you're serious about your future, why would you spend less time preparing for a career than most people spend on the job? Right now this *is* your job, and how you prepare will make the difference between success and failure.

Most educators will tell you that hard work, motivation, and extra effort can more than make up for less talent and intelligence. For most of us, nothing worth having or worth doing comes easily, and that includes learning. But if you really want better grades, and the rewards that come with them, then working hard and learning what it takes to truly learn, will make you a success not only in school but in whatever you choose to do in life.

2

Taking Notes

"If you hear a voice within you say that you cannot paint
then by all means paint, and that voice will be silenced."
- Vincent Van Gogh, 1853-1890

Unless you have a photographic memory, it's virtually impossible to remember everything you see or hear in a lecture. Besides, speakers have very different lecture styles. Some are prepared, well-organized, and crystal clear; others drone on, get off topic, or are so boring that you have to force your eyelids to stay open. Good note-taking can often compensate for a poor lecture. It helps you focus on the material and select the information that's important rather than trying to write down every word that's being said.

The purpose of taking notes is to help you outline critical ideas, especially those that the lecturer thinks are important. Taking notes forces you to listen more carefully. Because they're a summary of what you just spent an hour listening to, they need to be legible, efficient, and concise. A good note-taker prepares for the lecture beforehand, uses effective note-taking techniques during the lecture, and then reviews and rewrites notes after the lecture. Good note-taking helps you to use in-class time wisely and to get the most out of every lecture.

What to Do Before Class

The most important note-taking strategy happens before you even walk into a lecture. Nothing is more frustrating than not understanding what a teacher is talking about or frantically trying to write down every word the teacher says. At the end of the lecture, you walk out with pages of notes but little understanding of what they mean because you'd been too busy writing instead of listening. Here are some tips on what to do before a lecture in order to make note-taking as efficient as possible:

1. **Read and review the material beforehand.** Getting a general feel of what the lecture will be about is half the battle. By having at least some knowledge of the material, you'll be able to concentrate better and anticipate important concepts and ideas.

2. **Familiarize yourself with key words and concepts.** As you read, jot down unfamiliar terms and then look them up before class. When you hear them during the lecture, you'll recognize them and won't be so distracted.

3. **Bring a list of questions.** Once you've read the chapter, write down some questions you might want to ask the instructor. Listen for the answers and explanations during the lecture; and if your questions aren't answered, ask them at the end.

A good way to summarize or outline what's contained in a chapter is to use what's called "mapping," which should only be one page in length and be included at the beginning of your other notes. The advantages of mapping are that you're breaking the chapter down into smaller parts and you'll remember more because you'll be actively rather than passively reading. Here's a mapping example from a chapter on Earth Science:

Text: Environment and Man

Chapter 10

In Quest of Energy

A. Introduction, pp 203-205

B. Coal, pp 205-208

    a. Coal reserves in the United States

    b. Coal gasification for producing high energy methane

    c. Fluidization process for gasification of coal

    d. Magnetohydrodynamics for power generation

C. Oil, pp 208-211

    a. Oil reserves in the U.S. and foreign countries

    b. Synthetic fuels, oil sands, and oil shale

D. Natural Gas, pp 211-212

    a. Importance in the energy market

    b. Methods for natural gas extraction

E. Nuclear Power, pp 212-217

    a. Light water nuclear reactors and their operations

    b. Breeder reactors: advantages and disadvantages

    c. Nuclear fusion and its role in commercial energy

F. Water Power, pp 218-220

    a. Potential as a viable energy source

    b. Tidal power: advantages and disadvantages

G. Geothermal Energy, pp 220-224

    a. Areas of main production in the U.S.

    b. Geothermal steam plants and their operations

H. Solar Energy, pp 225-228

    a. Solar heating and cooling systems

    b. Solar power plants and their operations

Mapping can really help get things rolling because you're building a road map of the chapter and you're actively involved in reading. More importantly, you'll be in the study mode even before you hear the lecture, and that in itself will make the lecture more interesting and much easier to follow.

How to Take Notes During the Lecture

Every note-taking system has one thing in common: to provide you with an easy-to-read outline of information you'll need to study, review and learn. But regardless of which method you choose, you need to be flexible. Change your note-taking system to fit various lecture types or if it's not working for you. The bottom line is that your note-taking must help you learn and result in better grades. Here are two of the most popular methods.

Formal Outline System

The formal outline is a simple system of writing down main ideas or concepts and then listing important facts, dates, and key points pertinent to those ideas. The general outline would look like this:

Title of Topic

    A. Main idea or concept

        a. Pertinent information about idea

            i. key point

           ii. key point

          iii. key point

        b. Pertinent information about idea

            i. key point

           ii. key point

    B. Second main idea or concept

        a. Pertinent information about idea

            i. key point

           ii. key point

    C. Third main idea or concept

        a. Pertinent information about idea

           Etc.

When using this system, it's important to listen for main ideas and key concepts. By reading the material beforehand, and mapping the chapters, you'll easily pick up these ideas and concepts during the lecture. Here's an actual example of what a page of student notes might look like following a lecture on Management Hierarchy:

Topic: Management Hierarchy

A. Industry: A system composed of technology and an executive and administrative bureaucracy

    a. Bureaucracy includes levels of workers

        i. white collar – executives and managers

        ii. blue collar – production workers

    b. Functions of corporate management executives

        i. decision-making at a policy level

        ii. coordination and troubleshooting

        iii. maintaining favorable relations between the organization and consumers

    c. Middle management is between blue collar and corporate executives. Includes:

        i. vice presidents – implement and carry out decisions made at the top

        ii. specialists – professionals trained in a narrow field of specialization who deal with one aspect of production

        iii. foreman – implement decisions that have already been made

        iv. office workers – position is below specialists and whose role is similar to blue collar worker who have a higher status

Cornell Note-taking System

This method of note-taking is popular because it's simple to use and easy to study from. It's a little more detailed than the formal system in that you record a variety of information such as ideas, details, vocabulary, diagrams or charts, and examples. It's also flexible enough to use with just about any type of instructor and any kind of lecture.

When using the Cornell method, use a 3-ring loose leaf binder and draw three lines as shown in the diagram. The loose leaf binder allows you to add handouts and notes from other sources. Use the upper section to write the course name, the date, and the page number. The left side is used to record main points and ideas while the right side is used for writing down important information that supports or explains the main topics, which might be single words or phrases that the instructor emphasizes. The bottom of the page is a summary. Listen for vital cues such as "the main point is" or "the reason for this is," etc. The following is the Cornell page format and an example of a student's notes:

Subject / Topic / Date	
Cue Column	Main Notes Column
Summary Section	

Biology 100 – Biological Molecules – September 4th	
Bio Molecules	Carbohydrates, Lipids, Proteins, Nucleic Acids
Carbohydrates (CHO)	Short-term energy source; contain carbon hydrogen and oxygen; 3 types: Monosaccharaides – simple, single sugars, ex. glucose and fructose Disaccharides – 2 sugars linked together, ex. sucrose and lactose Polysaccharides – many sugars linked together, ex. starch and glycogen
Lipids	Long-term source of energy; 2x as many calories as CHO; 3 types: Oils and Fats – glycerol + 3 fatty acids Phospholipids – glycerol + 2 fatty acids and a phosphate; important in cell membranes Steroids – composed of 4 rings and made from cholesterol; ex. estrogen and testosterone
Proteins	Composed of amino acids 20 different amino acids are either: essential A.A. – need to get in the diet non-essential A.A. – body makes these so you don't need to eat them A.A. are linked together forming peptide bonds
Nucleic Acids	DNA & RNA Contained in the nucleus Blueprints for telling body how to make proteins

Summary: Living organisms are made up of 4 types of biological molecules. CHO are used for short-term energy, lipids are used for long-term energy, proteins are used as building blocks in the body, and nucleic acids are the blueprints that tell the body how to make proteins.

The Cornell system involves five steps designed to make study and learning as efficient as possible. They are:

1. **Record your notes.** Write short sentences or phrases in the right hand column as you listen to the lecture. Leave the left cue column empty until after class. It's helpful to use abbreviations and other short-hand symbols that make sense to you, as well as diagrams and charts.

2. **Reduce your notes.** As soon after class as possible, write key words or short phrases in the left cue column that will help you remember the information you wrote in the main notes area. As you write in the cue column, ask yourself questions that will trigger learning and help you prepare for exams. The summary section on the bottom of the page is meant to summarize only that page and not the entire lecture.

3. **Recite your notes.** Reciting your notes aloud as you reduce them into the cue column will help you think more deeply about the material. The physical act of listening to yourself recite your notes will be a second pathway through which information gets into your brain.

4. **Reflect on your notes.** As you recite your notes, ask yourself questions such as "What does this mean? How does this relate to the rest of the material? What is the significance? Do I understand this?" True learning and creativity comes only through reflection, so don't discount the value of this step.

5. **Review your notes.** Spend time every day, even if it's ten or fifteen minutes, reviewing your notes. This is much better and more effective than cramming for hours the night before an exam. By continually looking at your notes, you'll keep them fresh in your mind and retain the information more easily.

As soon as you walk into a classroom, begin preparing yourself for the lecture. Never go in with a negative attitude because you might not like the instructor or the subject matter, and never tell yourself that "This is going to be boring." That kind of negative self-talk sets the stage for poor listening and a short attention span. Instead, go over your notes from the last lecture and the questions you've written down for the new lecture. This automatically gets your brain focused for concentration and learning.

Listening is a skill that needs to be learned. When you listen well, you can concentrate when a discussion goes off topic or when a speaker is really bad. During a lecture, there are certain things you can do that will help you keep focused, stay on track and take good notes no matter what. Here are some suggestions:

- **Begin each lecture on a new page.** Every lecture should have its own notes, beginning on a separate page with the date and topic written at the top. Use only one side of the paper when taking notes; and if there are handouts or other type of materials, you can include them on the opposite side of the note book from the actual note-taking page it corresponds to.

- **Make your notes legible and brief.** Try to make your notes as brief and as legibly as possible. Don't write long sentences when you can use short phrases, words, or symbols that you can understand. Otherwise you'll be so worried about writing down every word that you miss half of what's being said.

- **Leave gaps between main ideas.** Leaving some space between lines allows you to go back and fill in the blanks during your review. If you miss something, you can look it up later and add it to your notes.

- **Develop a system for abbreviating.** Use abbreviations and symbols whenever you can. They can be standard abbreviations or a system you develop yourself and that flows easily when the instructor is talking too fast. For example, if the entire lecture is on China, use Ch for China, c for communism, gov. for government, etc. General notes can be in your own words, but things like formulas, definitions, rules, specific facts, and drawings must be written down exactly.

- **Include all the instructor's examples and illustrations.** If an instructor thinks that lecture material is important enough for him/her to stop and write it on the board or to slow down and give an example, then it's important enough for you to write it down as completely as possible. This is especially true if the instructor repeats the information. As a teacher, I'm not going to waste class time repeating material that I don't think is important enough to include on my next exam.

The Cornell system of note-taking is effective because it's simple and efficient. It allows you flexibility and a way to take notes that you can then rewrite, expand on, and review. Most importantly, this system is a proven method for helping you stay focused during the lecture, which translates into better learning.

What to Do After the Lecture

What you do right after class or at least within 24 hours of the lecture is just as important as what you do before or during a lecture. In fact, experts on study skills consider post lecture review and editing the most important part of learning. The following suggestions will enhance the notes you take and increase your ability to learn the material.

- **Edit anything that's not legible.** Within a day of the lecture, sit down and go over your notes. Correct inconsistencies, fix errors, and clean up illegible writing while the material is still fresh in your mind. The longer you wait, the harder it is to remember what you've written. If necessary, talk to your instructor, your classmates, or consult your textbook and additional sources to clear things up.

- **Fill in the Cue Column.** After class is the time to complete the cue column. Here you'll add key words and phrases related to the material in the note-taking column. The cue column may also include charts, diagrams or images that help summarize specific ideas. Cover up the right side of the paper and the cue column can now be used as a study guide.

- **Fill in any blank spaces.** There will always be missing information after a lecture, and this is why it's important to leave enough space in your note-taking column to add material, include additional words, or complete sentences that don't make sense. Also, include additional details that will enhance what you've already written.

- **Review the material.** Retention falls off sharply the longer you wait to review. So within 24 hours, go over lecture notes so that you're not relearning material that you should be reviewing. This is also where your index cards come in so handy. By periodically using these flash cards to review, you'll always keep the material fresh in your mind.

- **Rewrite your notes.** Proponents of the Cornell System say that rewriting notes is not necessary, but I don't think it's ever a waste of time to rewrite your notes. I did it for every one of my classes. In fact, the very act of rewriting is really your first review. If you're going to spend several hours studying from your notes anyway, why not add an extra dimension to your learning?

  If nothing else, rewriting is active learning. It gets you involved more than simply reading or editing. Finally, a clean set of notes without a lot of marks, scribbles, smudges, lines and cross-outs will make study easier because you won't have to fight through a maze of corrections.

Advice for Non-English Students

It's hard enough for many students to follow a lecture and take notes as it is; for students with non-English backgrounds, it's especially difficult and frustrating. Even if the instructor is speaking clearly and at a normal pace, it still seems too fast and confusing. Here are some suggestions that will help:

- **Record lectures.** This often helps English-speaking students; it will certainly help those who have trouble understanding the instructor. Later, when you're reviewing your notes, you can go back and listen to the recorded lecture as often as you like. Make sure you ask the instructor's permission before recording.

- **Practice listening.** As much as you can, listen to spoken English, whether it's on TV, the radio, or to other students. Watching TV shows will help you learn pronunciations and some of the peculiarities of the language. Also, listening to your recorded lecture several times will be helpful.

- **Read in advance.** Preparing for the lecture by familiarizing yourself with the material and with new words will make listening to it easier. Keep a dictionary handy and refer to it as often as you can.

- **Keep a separate page(s) with new words.** At the back of your notes, keep a list of words specific to the subject, along with their definitions, that are giving you trouble.

There's a good correlation between good note-taking and success on exams. Of course it takes more than good notes to be a good student, but as a teacher I can say that note-taking is a significant part of the learning process. Students who do well on my exams are usually the ones who don't miss class and have a well-developed system of taking notes. They review regularly, ask questions, and study actively, often coming to me in order to clarify something in their notes they might not understand. Good note-taking skills may not be the most important ingredient in your recipe for success, but it's a skill that will guarantee better grades no matter what subject you're studying.

3

Memory Techniques & Strategies

"Only those who will risk going too far can
possibly find out how far one can go."
- T.S. Eliot, 1888-1965

Most of us have spent a lot of extra hours studying for an exam simply because we had problems memorizing the material. Whether you like it or not, certain subjects like History and Geography require you to recall numbers, facts, dates, or other information. The good news is that memorizing these things is a learned skill and that the more you try to remember things, the more you exercise your brain and the easier it will be to remember the next time. Developing a system for memorizing will jump start your study sessions and make your school life a lot easier.

Memory and Observation

One of the most important elements in memory is the ability to observe. Without observation, we have nothing to input into our brain. Imagine a detective at the scene of a crime who walks into a room and only looks at the body of the victim without noticing anything else around him. He'd go back to the precinct and not have very much to report on other than that the victim was lying in the middle of the room.

The same thing often happens when you read or try to memorize something. You might get through an entire page only to realize that you have no idea what you'd just read. Maybe you were thinking about something else, or listening to a song on the radio, or watching a TV show. Whatever it was, it was enough of a distraction that your mind was not focused and you missed the point of the article you were reading.

To improve your observational skills and, therefore, your memory, all you need to do is make a conscious effort to observe. It sounds simple, but many students really need to do this to prevent thinking about other things and having their minds wander. Tell yourself beforehand that you're going to observe. Unless you make a real effort to observe everything, no memories will form that link to what you're trying to learn.

Mnemonics

The term mnemonic comes from a Greek word that means to remember. Basically it's any device that helps us recall information, and it could be a word, a short phrase, a list, a song, or even a visual or auditory cue. Mnemonics rely on links between what we already know and what we need to remember. This is based on the fact that our mind can more easily remember personal, physical, sexual, exaggerated, vivid, or humorous information than more arbitrary or abstract things.

One of the problems we face when we study is that our brains have evolved a way of interpreting and storing stimuli like smell, taste, touch, vision, and hearing, but when it comes to remembering words on paper, it doesn't do as well. The other problem is that some of us are either right-brained or left-brained, which makes it difficult to remember certain subjects because we're not naturally inclined to find those subjects easy to learn. Along comes mnemonics, which uses the brain's ability to interpret difficult-to-remember information to help us remember just about anything.

Before I talk about various types of mnemonics and memory techniques, the following are some ways to really make them much more effective:

- **Use colors to stimulate the senses.** Color is a great stimulant, so try to imagine things in color rather than in black and white.

- **Don't use negative images.** Your brain is programmed to be more receptive to positive thoughts and images so don't use a mnemonic that's unpleasant or negative.

- **Make your images move.** Actions trigger memory more so than static images. As you try to memorize something, make it move, give it life, and add some zest to your images.

- **Make your images funny or ridiculous.** The funnier, bizarre, sexy, and/or more ridiculous you make your image, the more likely you'll remember it. Add some action to the funny image and it'll be even more memorable.

- **Exaggerate size and shape.** Make your images bigger than life or exaggerate one or more of the main features. This goes hand in hand with making your images funny, bizarre, or ridiculous.

- **Use all of your senses.** The best mnemonics are ones that contain movements, smells, sounds, tastes, and feelings. Your senses are powerful tools that can condition your brain to remember things and then trigger recall.

For a mnemonic device to work well for a specific topic and be as powerful as it can be, use ideas and images from your own personal experiences and make good use of your imagination. Think back to your childhood and remember how much fun it was to imagine silly things. Imagination creates strong images that are memorable, but if you use images that are familiar to you they'll be much stronger and even more memorable. I can remember mnemonics that I'd used 40 years ago as if I were still a college freshman. That's how powerful these memory aids can be when used the right way.

Simple Mnemonic Devices

Probably the simplest way to remember something is to use a device we're all familiar with ever since we started school, and that is to use a sentence with the first letter of each word acting as a cue for what you need to remember. These devices have been standard memory techniques for many years because they're simple and they work.

One example would be if you wanted to remember that the steps of cell division, in order, are: Interphase, Prophase, Metaphase, Anaphase, and Telophase. In this case, just make a sentence like **I** **P**ray **M**ondays **A**nd **T**uesdays. To remember the order of the planets Mercury, Venus, Earth, Mars, Jupiter, Saturn, Uranus, Neptune, Pluto, you might use a sentence like **M**y **V**ery **E**xcited **M**other **J**ust **S**erved **U**s **N**ine **P**ickles. Or how about in taxonomy, when you need to remember **K**ingdom, **P**hylum, **C**lass, **O**rder, **F**amily, **G**enus, **S**pecies? You might use a sentence like **K**ing **P**hilip **C**uts **O**pen **F**ive **G**reen **S**nakes.

Another effective method is to use a single word as an acronym, with each letter representing the idea you must recall. For example, **BRASS** may be the acronym for the steps you need to go through when shooting a rifle: **B**reath, **R**elax, **A**im, **S**ight, and **S**queeze. If you need to remember the five Great Lakes, which are Huron, Ontario, Michigan, Erie, and Superior, use a word likes **HOMES**. Of course everyone knows that **FACE** represents musical notes on the spaces between lines.

Whatever word you choose, make sure it's one that you'll remember easily. Sometimes a common word is not as effective as one that sounds strange or is somehow related to what you're trying to memorize. Use your imagination and go with what works best for you.

Number/Shape Mnemonic

You'll often be asked to remember a list of things, whether they're in a particular sequence or not. This requires that you use a set of images associated with numbers, each number having a specific shape or mental hook. This mental hook is then used to link any other image you want. As an example, the following 10 images are associated with the numbers one through ten. Remember these or choose your own images.

Number	Mental Image
1	A flickering birthday **CANDLE** shaped like a one
2	A **COBRA** in the strike position that looks like a two
3	A **TREE** (sounds like three)

4	A **GOLFER** yelling "**FORE**" (sounds like four)
5	A **LARGE HAND** with five really fat fingers
6	A bunch of **BROOM STICKS** (sounds like six)
7	A pair of **DICE** showing seven or craps
8	A **FIGURE SKATER** doing a figure eight
9	A **CAT** with nine lives
10	A **FAT TENOR** singing an opera (sounds like ten)

These are the images I chose because I thought they would stick in my mind the most. You should choose your own personal images, but make them vivid and easy to remember, and never change them. The more you use them, the more they'll become ingrained in your memory.

Now, let's say you need to learn the first 10 amendments to the Constitution. Using the mental images associated with numbers one through ten will make this fairly easy. Take one amendment at a time and visualize the most vivid, unusual, or ridiculous scene you can come up with that links the number image with the amendment. This is how I did it:

First Amendment: Freedom of religion, speech, the press, and peaceful assembly.
Mental image: A giant number one candle sticking out of the ground, its light shining down on a group of assembled people who are praying, speaking, and reading newspapers.

Second Amendment: Right to keep and bear arms.
Mental image: A large cobra (shaped like a two) wearing an army helmet and holding a rifle.

Third Amendment: No soldiers may be quartered in private homes.
Mental image: A giant oak tree outside a private home. British soldiers are perched on its branches, not allowed into the home.

Fourth Amendment: No unreasonable searches and seizures.
Mental image: A crazed golfer yelling "fore" and then storming into a home looking for and seizing his golf ball.

Fifth Amendment: The right to a grand jury and the right to remain silent to prevent incrimination.
Mental image: A giant hand inside a courtroom holding a grand jury, and all the jurors holding their five fingers over the mouth of a defendant to keep him quiet.

Sixth Amendment: The right to a speedy and public trial.
Mental image: Broom sticks prodding a judge to speed up the trial in front of a crowd.

Seventh Amendment: The right to trial by jury.
Mental image: A giant pair of dice rolling into a courtroom and settling into the juror's box.

Eighth Amendment: No cruel or unusual punishment.
Mental image: A figure skater locked up in a filthy, rat infested prison, with only bread and water, is skating on a concrete floor, making the figure eight.

Ninth Amendment: Protects individual rights not directly mentioned in the Constitution.
Mental image: A cat dressed in a 3-piece suit, walking up the steps of Congress and demanding that he has rights too, even though cats are not mentioned in the Constitution.

Tenth Amendment: States are given powers not delegated to the federal government.
Mental image: A 10,000 foot fat tenor stands on a map of the United States; and while he sings he reaches over and takes electrical power stations from Washington and puts them in his state.

The beauty of this memory system is that once you've memorized the number images, you'll remember items even if they're out of order. Most students couldn't tell me who the eighth president of the United States was, but after visualizing a figure skater on top of a large bureau or a minivan, they will immediately say President Van Buren. The more you use and practice this system, the easier it will be to visualize a scene and remember it. As you get better at it, add mental images and expand your number collection.

Using Imaging to Remember

Of all the senses in your body, the sense of sight is the most perceptive and responsive you have. In fact, for most students, the information they remember best is information that they see, not what they hear. So to add permanence to your memory, you need to produce vivid mental images that will be ingrained in your mind. The two important rules to follow for effective visualization are:

- **Make your images as vivid and as exaggerated as possible.** The more ludicrous, unusual, ridiculous or larger-than-life your image is, the more unforgettable it will be. Think about the pictures you've seen over the years. The ones that had the most impact are probably the ones that made you laugh uncontrollably or ones that shocked or saddened you. The more extraordinary the image, the longer you'll remember it.

- **Try to make your images move.** Action scenes will generally leave a more lasting impression than static scenes and will remain with you much longer. If you're a movie or television lover, you know that what you see on TV or in the movies will leave a stronger impression on you than still photos will. Also, the movies that most likely had the greatest impact on you were ones that were the most graphic or the funniest.

A great way to remember facts is to come up with an image that you'll associate with the fact. How, for example, would you remember that Frankfort is the capital of Kentucky? The first thing to do is search your knowledge base. You know that Kentucky is the bluegrass state and is famous for thoroughbred race horses. So if you want to remember that Frankfort is the capital city of Kentucky, picture in your mind a big, fat, giant frankfurter inside a bun grazing on a blue pasture next to thoroughbreds.

The more ridiculous the picture, the better it is. Try it. Close your eyes and imagine a hotdog the size of a horse grazing on blue grass. Keep that image in your mind a few seconds and then forget it. A week later, ask yourself what the capital of Kentucky is and that image will pop into your head immediately.

Here are some more examples. When remembering that Santa Fe is the capital of New Mexico, picture a big fat **Santa** Claus delivering **new** presents to **Mexican** American children in the middle of the hot desert. Or when learning that Brussels is the capital of Belgium, you can picture a giant bell inside a gym (**bell** + **gym**) made of **Brussels** sprouts. To this day, my wife, who was having trouble remembering that the Carpathian Mountains are the major mountain chain in Poland, just pictures a Polish psycho**path** driving his **car** wildly over the tops of mountains and she instantly remembers it even after 30 years. By making the image animated and silly, you'll remember it.

The Story Method

This mnemonic device is an effective way to remember simple lists by linking items in a list with vivid images in a story that you tell yourself. The scenes become a motion picture in your mind. Begin by creating a link between the first item on your list and the next item. The story continues as each item is then linked one by one in a set of scenes that lead you through the images.

Try practicing this method with a grocery list the next time you go shopping. Write down a list of items, visualize a scene using each item to trigger the next, and then try to recall the items in order without looking at your list. For example, if your list includes eggs, milk, bread, paper towels, carrots, lettuce and hot dogs, picture this scene: **Eggs** fly out of a **milk** container and splatter all over a loaf of **bread**. The bread wipes itself off with **paper towels**, which it throws on the floor. Along comes a bunch of **carrots** that trip over the paper towels and falls into a head of angry **lettuce** that's having a picnic and eating **hot dogs**. The sillier the scene is, the more unforgettable it is.

Here's another example of how you might remember the first five presidents of the United States: Washington, Adams, Jefferson, Madison, and Monroe. Picture a **washing** machine dressed in a colonial outfit. Along comes a very hairy **Adam** from the Garden of Eden to remove his loincloth from the wash. He opens the washer door and out fly hundreds of **Jiffy** peanut butter jars instead. The jars are all over the floor, hopping **mad** that they were put in the machine. They run out, grab a giant **main** street sign and **row** away on it.

Here again, you make the scene as silly as possible so that it sticks in your mind. Also, make the images flow seamlessly so that one scene automatically triggers the next. The more you practice this technique, the better you'll get at coming up with a motion picture that will leave a lasting impression in your mind.

The Roman Room System

The Roman room system has been around a very long time. Basically this memory technique, also called the Loci method, has you create a mental picture of a room, typically your home or any room that you're intimately familiar with and then, as you walk around the room, link items in the room with a list of things you need to remember in no particular order. To recall information, you begin by visualizing the items you know well and linking them with images of whatever you need to memorize. The two main rules when using this method are:

- **Imprint the room and its contents in your mind.** Close your eyes and take some time to really get to know your room. Spend an hour or more if you need to, but make sure that your room is always the same and that the items are in the right places so that the process becomes ingrained.

- **Make the images you want to remember vivid and active.** The livelier, more exaggerated, and more ridiculous the image you want to remember is, the more likely it will be that you'll remember it.

As an example, imagine that your living room has the following items: coffee table, sofa, bookcase, lamp, television, stereo, mirror, and painting. These are you peg images. And then let's say that you need to remember that the five classes of vertebrates are fish, amphibians, reptiles, birds, and mammals. As you walk into the living room, you image fish flopping around on your coffee table. You then see two giant frogs sitting and kissing on your sofa. When you look at your bookcase, you see hundreds of snakes slithering out from between the books. Next to the bookcase, you imagine your lamp and see a large eagle flying out from beneath the lampshade. Finally, you look at the television and see several monkeys fighting over the remote control.

The technique works best when the room and the items are familiar to you and if the images are as ridiculous and animated as they can be. You can expand this system by adding doors through which you walk through and go into other rooms that contain more familiar items that you can use as pegs.

Remembering Through Inferences and Analogies

An effective way to make new and unfamiliar information more meaningful and more likely to be remembered is through inferences and analogies. This involves thinking about the information, ideas, or opinions and drawing conclusions from that new information. For example, if you're reading about a new invention, you might think about how it changed people's lives and habits at the time of the invention. Or when studying the circulatory system, you might think about how diet, activity, or illness can affect it.

Creating inferences forces you to think about what you're studying. You become an active rather than a passive learner. And being active in your learning keeps your mind from wandering and enhances your concentration. This, in turn, increases your ability to store information into long-term memory. The very act of making inferences while reading or studying stimulates brain cells and will increase your capacity to learn. Analogies are similarities between things that are otherwise not alike. You create the most effective analogies when you compare new material with material you already know well.

Here's an example: suppose you're trying to learn the differences between arteries in the human body, which are large blood vessels that have great pressure and carry oxygen-rich blood out to the body's organs and tissues, and veins, which are much thinner, have low pressure, and carry oxygen-poor blood back to the heart. One way to think about this is to make a simple plumbing analogy.

Think of the water as blood, the pipes under the sink as veins, the faucet as a heart and arteries, and the sink as the body. The water (blood) comes out of the faucet (heart and arteries) with great force and carries it out to the sink (body). The water (blood) is used in the sink (body), leaves, and drains in the pipes (veins) with much less force before it goes to the water treatment plant and back to the faucet (heart).

Another way to help remember through inferences and analogies is to us a double entry journal with two columns. On one side you write down what the text is saying; on the other side you write down what it makes you think of.

Creating analogies builds a mental bridge between what you already know and what you need to learn. With a little practice, anyone can think of situations or visualize images that make analogies for whatever is being learned. Because your brain responds well to this kind of technique, use it often and you'll see how much more your study sessions improve.

Remembering Through Review

Regular review of your study material is absolutely essential for proper recall. Even if you become an expert in memory techniques, you still have to reinforce the information stored in your memory through periodic review. The following are some proven strategies for using review as a memory tool.

- **Go over lecture material every day.** Most forgetting occurs shortly after learning has taken place. By not allowing too much time to pass between the time you get the information and the time you review it, you'll reinforce what's in your head.

- **When reviewing, have a pen or pencil in your hand.** Actively review by jotting down key ideas, principles, concepts, and questions you think might be on the next exam. If necessary, draw diagrams, charts, and illustrations since pictures make the information more vivid and understandable.

- **Have a cumulative review every week.** Each week, go back and review previous material, which will not only reinforce what you've already learned, it will help you understand new material. Use the flash cards that you've been accumulating for additional reinforcement.

- **Read your notes out loud.** When reviewing, use as many of your senses as possible. Information that you input into your brain through both your eyes and your ears is going to be stored more easily than information you only read. Add to that some rewriting and you're really using your senses in the most effective way possible.

- **Categorize review material.** When reviewing large amounts of information, it helps to group it into categories. For example, when reviewing for a Zoology exam, study animals after dividing them into groups such as reptiles, mammals, fish, birds, amphibians, etc. If you're learning about musical instruments, it helps to organize them into strings, brass, woodwinds, and percussion. It's much easier to remember several smaller groups of related items than to remember one large group.

- **Review in short rather than long sessions.** Memory is significantly increased when information is spread out over several short days rather than one long day. A famous study found that it took individuals 68 repetitions to remember information they were given, but when spread out over a 3-day period, the individuals needed only 38 repetitions to remember the same information. That's a fifty percent reduction in work.

- **Before exams, lecture to yourself from your notes.** While reviewing, become the teacher and lecture to your imaginary class as you review. Try to imagine that you're explaining the material to students as if they were hearing it for the first time. Remember, we learn 90% of what we teach to others.

Foods that Boost Brainpower and Memory

To maximize memory and brainpower, you need proper nutrients to feed your brain cells. But can certain foods actually make you smarter? Research had shown that it's true; that you can become more alert, increase your concentration, and improve your memory by eating the following brain-boosting foods:

Omega-3 fatty acids: The brain's gray matter is composed in part of omega-3 fatty acids. So to maintain proper nerve function and to enhance memory, eat fish (wild-caught salmon), olive oil, beans, walnuts, almonds, and flax seed.

Berries: The antioxidants in berries such as blueberries, cranberries, strawberries, blackberries, and raspberries decrease free radical damage and boost memory.

Cruciferous and green leafy vegetables: Studies have shown that cruciferous vegetables like broccoli, Brussels sprouts, and cauliflower, and green leafy vegetables like spinach, kale, and Swiss chard have a great effect on helping you retain memory.

Folic acid: Found in foods such as eggs, whole grains, lentils, soybeans, spinach, green peas, beets, and oranges, folic acid has a direct effect on memory and fast information processing.

Tubers: To nourish brain cells and increase brain power, eat more sweet potatoes, carrots, and beets. These foods are rich in Vitamin B, C, and beta-carotene.

Beans: To help with attention, problem solving, and memory, your brain needs thiamin or Vitamin B1. Beans such as lima beans, green beans, black beans, lentils, and kidney beans have more thiamine than just about any other food.

Some Final Tips for Improving Memory

Hopefully, the techniques in this chapter will help jump start your brain power and consequently your learning. They're not difficult, but they do require some effort on your part if you want them to be as effective as they can be. Here are some final suggestions on getting the most out of your memory power:

- **Make a conscious decision to remember.** This obvious point is often overlooked, but it's the first step to effective memory. Tell yourself that you'll remember. Before a lecture, say "I'm going to remember this material today." Most students don't go into a class planning to remember. In fact many walk in with a negative attitude, which makes it tough to learn anything.

- **Get enough sleep.** Learning, memorizing, and problem-solving are all compromised if you don't get enough sleep. For most of us, seven to nine hours is what's needed for our brains to function well. Some of us might need even more. In fact, experts tell us that the deepest stage of sleep is when our brain is working hardest to remember the things we experienced during the day. Also a good way to remember is to do a brief review an hour or so before bed and then sleep on it.

- **Learn to relax.** Experts tell us that 15 minutes of relaxation exercises or meditation is as effective as sleep. During a hectic semester, your mind needs to be fresh and sharp. Relaxation exercises and meditation will not only enhance your physical well-being, they'll increase your mental capacity as well. One surprising study found that students who were deprived of a full night's sleep but who meditated before an exam scored higher than students who slept well but didn't meditate.

- **Eat well-balanced meals.** Nutrients such as vitamins and minerals are essential for normal brain function and they prevent anemia, fatigue, and the inability to concentrate and learn. Students who don't eat well don't learn as well, and this is especially true during times of stress. The best brain-boosting diets are those low in saturated fats, high in colorful fruits and green leafy vegetables, and high in omega-3s such as cold water fish (salmon and sardines), walnuts, flaxseed, soybeans, and pumpkin seeds. A good multivitamin and a fish oil supplement is also a good idea.

- **Start an exercise program.** Individuals who exercise regularly are more alert, less sluggish, and have a better memory. There's a direct link between physical and mental health; so for maximum brain function start a regular exercise routine, even if it's just walking a few miles, three times a week. The extra blood flow during exercise will get more oxygen to your brain and significantly improve your mental function.

- **Stop multitasking.** You might think that you can study and learn just as well or even better listening to music or with the TV on, but you're just fooling yourself. Multitasking reduces your ability to learn and remember things because your brain is forced to switch over from the cerebral cortex, which is the main processing center for information to the striatum, which stores fewer details.

Since most of us aren't blessed with super memories, we have to rely on techniques and tricks that help our brain remember things. Just like a computer stores data, our brain often stores whatever we see and hear; but like a computer, it then hides it from us much like our losing access to one of our computer files. We know it's there; we just can't retrieve it.

Mental hooks, images, and cues are all very effective in getting at information that we know is there but needs to be jarred loose. The problem is not that we don't store information; it's that we can't access it. The more you use mnemonic techniques and follow the other suggestions for improving memory, the easier it becomes to remember. And once you begin to master the art of recall, your entire attitude about studying and learning will change because you'll discover that memory isn't necessarily something you're born with but a skill that you learn.

4

Improving Reading Skills

"It is not because things are difficult that we do not dare,
it is because we do not dare that things are difficult."
- Seneca, 3 B.C.E. – C.E. 65

When employers from different business sectors were asked what they look for most in potential applicants, the two qualities that stood out most were reading and writing skills. This was especially true for certain industries like business, healthcare, computer science, engineering, electronics, and manufacturing. As more of these careers become high tech, they require above average reading skills; and that means reading not only with speed but with comprehension. Students who improve their reading will dramatically improve their ability to learn and automatically improve their grades as a result. As an added benefit, they will be the ones most in demand by future employers.

Good readers are typically good learners because they have the ability to get at important information and process it in their brains. They're also efficient at what they read, gleaning facts and skimming over material that's not as critical. Knowing what to skip over is often just as important because it helps you focus and manage your time. So to read more effectively and with more comprehension and understanding, you need to do four things:

- Follow roadmaps within the chapters

- Read actively rather than passively

- Increase speed through daily practice

- Enhance vocabulary to increase comprehension

Of all the skills a student masters, reading is probably the single most important in terms of success and productivity. Unless a student has good reading skills, studying math and science, analyzing problems, exploring history, or enjoying the world of art and literature becomes impossible. But once a student becomes a skillful reader, he or she transitions from someone who has simply learned to read to someone who is reading to learn. And that's really the goal; to develop the skills needed to become part of an increasingly literate global society.

Following Chapter Roadmaps

Textbook publishers use a format that makes 90 percent of the most important information easy to locate. However, if the material in a chapter is new, you can't expect to identify and remember the key points or concepts right away. That's like asking you to locate someone's address in a different city without a street map. You would have no means of relating the new address to streets you're not familiar with. A map provides you with cues that help you know that you're going in the right direction.

In the same way, a good textbook provides a map so that you can find your way through sometimes difficult material. The map is made up of three main sections: An **Introduction**, the **Headings**, and a **Summary**. Sometimes an overview is included at the beginning that explains the purpose of the chapter. The introduction tells you what the chapter will cover, while the summary serves as a final outline of the most important material that was covered. In between, the headings give you an idea of the main topics you're about to read. Here's how to approach each of these sections:

Introduction: Read this section of the chapter carefully. When written well, the introduction gives you a good idea of what's ahead. Pause for a moment after reading it and reflect on what the author's purpose is.

Headings: These are typically bold-faced, capitalized, or both. The headings tell you exactly what the particular section of the chapter includes and prepares you for the material you're about to read. If there are subheadings, try to link them to the main heading to get a sense of how the material is being presented. Pause between headings and think about the content and what you've finished reading.

Summary: Read the summary as carefully as you did the introduction. Here the author is repeating or emphasizing his or her ideas, main points or arguments. Pause for a few moments after reading the summary, think about what you've read, and try to incorporate the ideas in the summary with the chapter headings.

Many texts include pictures, charts, graphs, illustrations, and vocabulary terms in bold print. These often do more to help you understand the text than the written material, so don't overlook them. In fact, when selecting textbooks for my classes, I often choose ones with the best illustrations and graphics because I know how much this helps students with their reading. Some of my students have told me that they look over the illustrations before they even read the text because they can get a better idea of what they're about to read when they use these visual aids prior to their reading and coming to class.

Besides the usual roadmaps, special type is sometimes placed within the text to draw your attention to important information. Don't ignore this, especially if the type is in boldface. If special type attracts your attention, it's because the material is worth going over carefully. This is part of an author's plan to emphasis a point or to make the material more readable. By getting in the habit of following the roadmaps that authors provide, you'll become an expert reader before you know it.

Reading Actively

After you preview the chapter and make sure you get a clear picture of what it is you're about to read, you're now in a better position to read actively. One of the most important things you want to do is find relationships between the material you read and your own knowledge base. This is what comprehension is all about.

To help you generate thoughts, and to keep your mind from wandering while you read, use the attention-focusing methods discussed in chapter one (self-talk, positive images, and questioning). Use information from the chapter preview to ask yourself questions that you expect to answer. Some students find it useful to pause before each new section of a chapter and use some of the main learning and memory aids, such as analogies, inferences, categorizing information, asking questions, finding main ideas, etc. to help them focus on and remember the material.

By creating analogies, making inferences, and asking questions, you know that you're doing more than just skimming the page; you're getting something concrete out of your reading. If you find yourself wondering what you just finished reading, you can be sure that your mind was somewhere other than on what you were reading. Refocus and get back to active reading.

One of the great things about using attention-focusing techniques is that you'll be elaborating on what you're reading and generating connections between what you already know or have experienced and what you read. This makes the material much more understandable and easier to remember because you're not waiting until you finish the entire section to elaborate.

Stopping to elaborate part way through the text is an effective method to increase comprehension and memory, but it also depends on the complexity of the subject. You may need to stop more often when reading a math or science text than you would when reading a history or sociology text. This active reading process is what keeps your mind on the task at hand.

Marking a textbook with a pencil or highlighter is an excellent way to help you read actively. Here are some ideas for making notes in your book while you read:

- **Underline main ideas.** Without getting too carried away, use a highlight pen to color important words and phrases. Highlighting is better than underling because it's usually not as distracting. Too much highlighting, on the other hand, can also be distracting.

- **Place asterisks in the margins next to important points.** If the asterisks are drawn in red or blue, they'll stand out more and draw your attention to the main points of the text.

- **Place numbers within the text next to lists of main ideas or important points.** When you do this, don't be so sloppy that your numbers cover up important words. Also, use a colored pen or pencil. Colors within the text will be more noticeable, and you won't have to read through the entire text to find a list of main points.

- **Circle new words to be learned.** When you come across new terms, circle them and make sure to look them up as soon as you can. In most cases, understanding the vocabulary terms is directly related to understanding the reading material.

- **Place notes in margins.** When reading, always have a pen or pencil in hand. The very act of jotting down notes and thoughts in the margins will get you actively involved in the reading process. Later, as you review, the thoughts you may have forgotten will be right there in the text along with the material.

When using these techniques, be careful not to cover up the words. Also, don't overdo it with the underlining or highlighting. Use too many lines and highlights and the ideas become lost among all the markings. The value of this system pays off when it's time to review because you won't have to reread page after page of text again. All the important information will be right there and easily located. So make active reading a habit and it will become a natural part of study and learning.

Reading for Comprehension

When you first learned to read, your reading comprehension was limited to single words. You associated a word with a sound or an object. As you progressed, you formed words into groups or phrases and then sentences. Once you were able to put those related sentences together to form a single idea within a paragraph, you were well on your way toward reading with comprehension.

Good readers go a step further. They take entire paragraphs and sections and link them together to get an overall understanding of what it is they're reading. To accomplish that you need to do three things: develop a good vocabulary, without which you can't really comprehend complex ideas and topics, recognize how authors are presenting the material, which involves previewing and mapping the chapter, and relating what you're reading to what you already know or have already experienced in other classes or in life.

The second factor in comprehension – recognizing how the author is presenting the material – is often overlooked. Whenever authors write a book, they break it down into introduction, body, and conclusion. Once they get you through the introduction, which should tell you what the chapter is about, authors use the body of the text to describe, explain, or discuss the material before summarizing it. The conclusion or summary is the author's final attempt at making the material clear. When reading the body of a text, here's what to look for:

Examples: Authors like to use various examples not only as a way to explain the material they're writing about, but also to hold the reader's attention. Look for examples immediately following explanations or discussions. They'll reinforce what you read and are often an important part of the book.

Definitions and illustrations: Within the body of the text, authors provide definitions and illustrations to elucidate ideas and main points. Never ignore these. Definitions explain what the author is talking about; and illustrations can be a better way to explain the material than the text itself. I often select text books based mainly on the quality of illustrations and how well they relate to the text. So as you read, pay particular attention to how the author is using an illustration to describe information.

Causes and effects: Whenever you read, try to figure out why something has caused something else to happen. For example, when an author is writing about the collapse of the former Soviet Union, you might ask yourself questions about the events that led up to the collapse or the factors that caused the circumstances leading up to the collapse. Doing this every time you read will make you a critical thinker as well.

Comparisons and contrasts: This technique is similar to making analogies. Authors using this technique are trying to compare what they're writing about to what they think you should already know. For example, when discussing the British system of government, an author may compare it to or contrast it with the American system of government. Pay special attention to this kind of writing.

The third factor in comprehension – relating what you're reading to what you know or have experienced – is a key element of active reading. You have to ask yourself how the information you just read compares to your experiences or the experiences of others. You must also ask yourself what the author is trying to say, what his or her objectives are, why the author has written the material in this manner, and why the author feels the way he or she does about the material.

By interpreting and analyzing information, you're really getting inside the author's head, which is precisely the point of active reading. Whenever you do this, your understanding improves and with it your ability to remember more of what you read.

Improving Vocabulary for Better Reading

Some years ago, one of my colleagues pointed out something to me that I found to be almost always true. He told me that a student often misses the main point or the meaning of a sentence because of one unfamiliar word. That one little word makes a student stop dead in his or her tracks and disrupts thought and concentration. It follows then that the better your vocabulary is the better your reading and comprehension will be. On the other hand, the more words you get stuck on as you read, the more frustrated you're going to be and the less you're going to want to continue reading. Vocabulary adds tremendous power to your learning. An added benefit is that you'll do much better on standardized tests, which assume a good knowledge of vocabulary.

There are many ways to improve your vocabulary. Go to any bookstore and you'll find a dozen good books on the subject, each one offering great techniques for learning new words. However, one of the best ways is to learn important prefixes and suffixes. These simple additions can give you the clues you need to decipher many words. The following are some proven strategies that have helped many students build a better, more functional vocabulary.

1. **Invest in a good dictionary.** Buy a good dictionary and keep it in a conspicuous place so that it's readily available. As you read, circle, underline, or mark words you don't know. Go back and look up those words. If it's a word you're really having trouble with, write it down

on an index card with the definition on the other side. Periodically, go through your cards to get those words in your long-term memory. You might also want to carry a small pocket dictionary with you at all times just in case. When you get in the habit of looking up definitions, you'll find that you can't pass up an unfamiliar word without having to know what it means.

2. **Read various magazines to add depth to your vocabulary.** Don't only read about things you're most interested in, even though reading what you like is a great way to enhance reading skills. The reason most students don't like to read about other things is that they encounter more unfamiliar words. So instead of avoiding certain topics because they're unfamiliar, make it a challenge to read a wide variety of topics so that your general vocabulary expands.

   A great way to improve the scope of your vocabulary is to subscribe to a magazine on a specific topic you really like and then supplement your reading with a few other magazines on topics that you normally wouldn't read about. For example, if you're really interested in science, subscribe to Scientific American, Nature, or Discover, but also read National Geographic, Newsweek, Time, the Atlantic, the New Yorker, etc. As you continue to read these magazines, unfamiliar words will appear more often and you'll quickly become familiar with them.

3. **Learn commonly used foreign words and phrases.** If you read different books and various types of materials, you're bound to come across some commonly used foreign words or expressions now and then. When you do, you might stop reading, scratch your head, and wonder why those foreign words or phrases were included in a book written in English. So to prevent confusion when you read, here are the most common foreign expressions you should know:

A priori: based on theory rather than observation. "The fact that he is eating everything in sight suggests *a priori* that he is very hungry."

Ad hoc: a special case. "Let's put together an *ad hoc* committee to decide on the proposal."

Ad infinitum: to infinity. "His speech is going on *ad infinitum*."

Ad nauseam: to a sickening degree. "She went on and on about her illness *ad nauseam.*"

Bona fide: in good faith. "This is a *bona fide* agreement."

Carte blanche: freedom to act on one's own. "You have *carte blanche* authority to buy whatever you want."

Cause célèbre: well known or controversial issue. "The new tax system voted in became a national cause célèbre."

Caveat emptor: let the buyer beware. "Before you buy that new television set from the street vendor, *caveat emptor.*"

Coup de grace: the final blow. "The *coup de grace* came with a grand slam in the bottom of the ninth inning.

Coup de tat: forcible overthrow of government. "Ten years of poverty finally led to a military *coup de tat.*"

De facto: official recognition. "After the votes were all counted in the election, the people recognized the socialist party as their *de facto* government."

Ex post facto: done afterwards, "The law was put into place *ex post facto.*"

Faux pas: social blunder. "Chewing with your mouth open is a serious *faux pas.*"

Fait accompli: a thing already done. "There's no use arguing about your exam grade; it's a *fait accompli.*"

Glasnost: openness. "Mikhail Gorbachev initiated *glasnost* in the Soviet Union in 1985."

In situ: in its original place. "As part of our experiment, the chemicals were placed in a test tube and mixed *in situ.*"

In toto: in full. "The loan was repaid *in toto.*"

Ipso facto: by the very fact. "A liar, *ipso facto,* cannot be an honest person."

Laissez faire: without interference. "A *laissez faire* attitude permeated the corporation run by young executives."

Nom de plume: pen name. "When writing, my *nom de plume* is W.J. Smith."

Nota bene: take notice. "*Note bene*. I am going out of town and will not be in tomorrow."

Par excellence: above all others. "The dinner was *par excellence*."

Per se: by itself. "The class *per se* is not interesting, but it's required.

Persona non grata: unwelcomed person. "When the war started, the diplomat was *persona non grata*."

Piece de resistance: the main dish or event. "The *piece de resistance* this evening will be the truffles."

Prima facie: at first sight. "Watching him steal the money was *prima facie* evidence of his guilt."

Pro bono: done for free. "The lawyer accepted the case *pro bono.*"

Quid pro quo: something for something or an equal exchange. "When she leant me the money I needed, I fixed her house *quid pro quo*."

Savoir-faire: knowing what to do or say. "In social circles, he had more *savoir-faire* than anyone else."

Sine qua non: indispensable element, action or ingredient. "Her very presence was the *sine qua non* of every dinner party."

Status quo: existing state of affairs. "The next election was meant to change the *status quo*."

Tour de force: feat of skill or strength. "His *tour de force* in this battle will be his skill with a sword."

Verboten: forbidden. "It is *verboten* to yell fire in a crowded theater."

Vis-à-vis: in relation to or in comparison with. "His profits were down *vis-à-vis* his expenses."

Vox populi: voice of the people. "When I win the election, I will listen to the *vox populi.*"

Zeitgeist: attitude of the times. "The *Zeitgeist* of the industrial revolution was that money was made at the expense of the individual."

4. **Learn the meaning of prefixes and suffixes.** A prefix is a syllable or word added at the beginning of another word in order to alter the meaning of that word or create a new one. A suffix is a syllable or word added at the end of a word to change that word's meaning or to create another word. Thousands of words are nothing more than a root word to which a prefix or suffix has been added. Knowing the meanings of the most common prefixes and suffixes will give you a good idea of a word's meaning. The following are lists of the most important ones:

Most Important Prefixes

A: not or without; *atypical* or not typical

Ante: preceding or before; *anteroom* or a room before another

Anti: against; *antidote* or a remedy against a poison

Auto: self; *autopilot* or self-flying aircraft

Contra: against or opposite; *contradict* or say the opposite

De: down; *devalue* or to bring down or lessen the value

Dis: remove, negate or expel; *dismantle* or remove something

Ex: out; *excavate* or to remove dirt when digging

Extra: outside or beyond; *extraterrestrial* or being from beyond earth

In: not; *inaudible* or not audible

Inter: between; *intermediate* or between two things

Mis: not or wrong; *misguided* or wrongly guided

Mono: one; *monologue* or speaking alone as one

Non: not; *nonessential* or not essential

Over: completely; *overzealous* or completely zealous

Post: after; *postpartum* or after birth

Pre: before; *preamble* or intro before the Constitution

Re: again; *recalculate* or to calculate over again

Super: above; *superimpose* or place over something

Trans: across; *transatlantic* or across the Atlantic

Un: not; *unarmed* or not armed

Uni: one; *unicycle* or one-wheeled bicycle

Most important Suffixes

Able, Ible: able to be or can be done; *comfortable* or able to have comfort

Ful: full of; *careful* or full of care

Less: without; *fearless* or without fear

Ly: characteristic of; *quietly* or the characteristic of doing something while being quiet

Ment: action or process; *enjoyment* or the process of enjoying

Ness: state of; *kindness* or the state of being kind

Ous: having qualities of; *joyous* or having the quality of joy

How to Increase Reading Speed

Although reading speed is often important, especially when you're pinched for time, not everything should be read quickly. This is true when you're reading about math or any kind of scientific information where you need to really focus on the material. So while reading quickly may be a good thing, you need to know when to kick it into high gear and when to slow down.

The average reader reads approximately 250 to 300 words per minute. Very good readers can double that. Anything faster is not going to be any more effective. The problem that average readers have is that when they need to slow down for difficult subjects, their speed drops down to below average. For example, a good reader covering 500 words per minute can slow down 50 percent and still be reading at a decent clip of 250 words per minute. And that's the advantage of speed reading – you'll have the skills needed to read anything quickly, but you don't have to worry about slowing down because you'll still be reading at a much faster rate than most people.

To increase reading speed, sometimes by as much as 100 percent, you must eliminate the physical habits that you might not even be aware you have and that are slowing you down. The five main ones are:

- Moving your lips while you read

- Moving your tongue, even if your lips are not moving

- Using your finger to point to words on a page

- Moving your head

- Rereading what you just read

These five habits can become so ingrained that it takes a real effort to eliminate them, especially if you've been doing them for a long time. Like any other habit, these are the result of conditioned behavior; and behavior can be changed with practice. Here are some strategies for reconditioning yourself to increase reading speed and become a more effective reader.

1. **Put something between your lips while you read.** If you put something between your lips, whenever you move them the object will bounce up and down, reminding you immediately not to be moving your lips. Another trick that often works is placing your finger gently across your closed lips and feeling for any movement as you read. By constantly being on guard for any movement, you'll quickly break the habit and won't have to pay attention to your lips again.

2. **As you read, place the tip of your tongue between your teeth.** You may not be moving your lips at all, but you may be verbalizing words with your tongue. This slows you down just as much because you're still saying every word to yourself. Placing your tongue between your teeth will keep you from doing this because when you try to verbalize, you'll feel yourself trying to pull your tongue out from between your teeth. This becomes annoying enough to help you break the habit.

3. **Hold the book your reading with both hands.** Holding a book with two hands keeps you from using your fingers to point to words. If you're lying down, you might put your free hand behind your head. If you're sitting, hold a cup or something else in your hand. Anything you can do to occupy those fingers will work.

4. **Place your hand against your head to prevent movement.** Moving your head isn't really that bad, but it can still slow you down. By resting your head against your immovable hand, you'll discourage any tendency to move as you read.

5. **Avoid the urge to go back and reread sentences or paragraphs.** You'd be surprised at how many students go back and reread a sentence or paragraph because they don't believe that they got everything the first time around. Research shows that that just isn't true, and that rereading may be cutting reading speed by as much as 50 percent. So when you feel the need to go back and read something over again, fight that urge and keep going. Before you know it, it'll seem like you're breezing right through the material. If you follow the suggestions about highlighting and writing in the margins, you won't feel the need to go back and reread because you'll know that you're going to be reviewing the material later anyway.

Techniques for Increasing Speed Reading

A key principle of speed reading is rapid eye movement. The faster your eyes move across a page, the more information you're going to be transmitting into your brain, up to a point. If you're not used to rapid eye movement, it is probably going to feel unnatural at first because you'll feel as if you're missing something. That's because you've conditioned yourself to search for single words rather than ideas or blocks or words. To increase speed, you have to recondition your mind to pick up increasingly larger segments of printed material. Once you do, your comprehension will also increase because you'll be taking in whole ideas rather than strings of individual words.

Another way to increase reading speed is to decrease the length of pauses between ideas or blocks of words. You may have developed the habit of excessive pausing when you were younger because you didn't have the confidence to know that you could pick up and absorb images much faster than you realize. Excessive pausing can also lead to rereading, since there's a tendency to go back after you pause to read something again. By eliminating pauses, you'll fight that urge to reread. The following are three suggestions for improving reading speed, which will also enhance reading comprehension.

1. **Use a training device such as an eye guide or ruler.** Make an eye guide by taking an index card and cutting out a slot the width of a magazine or newspaper column. Place the card over the column and move it smoothly down the page. Force yourself to pick up the entire line with your eyes without having to read each word. Gradually increase the speed at which you move the index card down the page. Another method is to simply use a ruler as a pacing guide. Place the ruler across the page and move it steadily downward as you read.

2. **Force your eyes to move over groups of words.** Good readers have trained themselves to take in as many words as possible by skipping across the page and taking in as many words as their eyes will allow. Here's what a poor versus a good reading pattern might look like:

Poor Reading Pattern

The / collapse / of / the / Soviet / Union / has / not / only / raised concerns / about / their / precarious / economy / but / about / their / vast nuclear / arsenal / as / well.

Good Reading Pattern

The collapse of the Soviet Union / has not only raised concerns / about their precarious economy / but about their vast nuclear arsenal as well.

3. **Spend 10 minutes a day reading as fast as possible.** Even if you don't think you comprehend what you're reading, you'll condition your eyes to see groups of words in short bursts. In no time at all, your brain will become conditioned to input visual images faster than you ever thought possible. By doing this exercise, your normal reading speed will seem so slow that you'll naturally want to speed up.

Some Final Tips for Improved Reading

Good readers read with both speed and comprehension. They look for ideas and main points within paragraphs, and they condition their eyes to pick up entire blocks of words rather than single words. They also eliminate habits like rereading and pausing, and they know when to slow down and speed up depending on the material they're reading. Here are some final suggestions that I found personally useful for students over the years.

- **Spend some of your daily leisure time reading.** Research shows that the amount of leisure time spent reading is directly related to reading comprehension, size of vocabulary, and gains in reading ability. This is especially true if you read a wide variety of subject matter, including fiction and non-fiction. So, instead of watching TV or playing that video game, spend time reading. You'll find that it gets to be a very enjoyable habit.

- **Don't read every subject in the same way.** In order to get the most from reading different subjects, you need to approach them differently. Here are some rules to follow:

Mathematics
a. Read slowly
b. Look for details and specific meanings
c. Use pencil and scratch paper to help you learn formulas and visualize concepts
d. Practice working problems at the end of each reading

Science
a. Read slowly to moderately
b. Look for relationships, main ideas, and causes and effects
c. Learn important Latin and Greek prefixes
d. Know the scientific method so that you read with more understanding
e. Never skip diagrams and illustrations

Social Sciences (History, Sociology, Economics, etc.)
a. Read moderately
b. Look for series of events and causes and effects between events
c. Learn commonly used language
d. Study charts, maps, and diagrams as you read

Literature
a. Read moderately to rapidly
b. Have a general idea of the plot by reading the introduction, preface, or author's notes

    c.   Ask yourself questions in order to follow the plot. "What's going on here? "What will happen next?" "Why is this happening?" etc.

    d.   Form opinions about what the author is trying to say or relate to you as the reader.

- **Look for signposts as you read.** There are certain words or groups of words that signal you to go ahead or to change direction. Both tell you to look out for upcoming ideas. Some go-ahead signals include: accordingly, also, as a result, furthermore, in conclusion, in fact, in summary, likewise, moreover, and subsequently. Changing direction signals include: although, despite, however, in spite of, on the contrary, notwithstanding, rather, regardless, and yet.

Based on years of teaching, I have to agree with many experts who say that without good reading skills students are doomed to mediocrity. If you can't read effectively, you can't develop the foundation necessary to get good grades. More importantly, you won't have the ability to learn what you need to know to become successful. It's true that the most successful students have the best reading habits; and if you want to transform yourself into a top student, read well and read often.

5

Improving Writing Skills

"There will come a time when you believe everything is finished . . .that will be the beginning."
- Louis L'Amour, 1908-1988

In today's world of computers, cell phones, text messages, and emails, many people are losing their ability to write. I see this with my students more and more each year. Grammar and spelling are taking a back seat to shortcuts that are becoming a part of our everyday language. And punctuation is something that is all but forgotten. Unfortunately, what students don't realize is that how they write will make an impression on admissions committees, future employers, and the people they work with who have to read their writing. One of the problems is that students get so used to writing in a certain way that they believe it will be accepted.

One of the most important aspects of writing is that by having the ability to present something in a clear, coherent, concise, and organized manner, you're actually making your life a lot easier. Rather than spending a lot of extra time thinking about how to write, you can think about what to write. So the better your writing skills are the more valuable you'll be and the more time you can devote to other things. You'll also get much better grades on exams and papers.

The Five Worst Writing Errors

Before we go on to other topics, let's get this one out of the way. Until you can identify some of these glaring problems, your writing will be mediocre at best and terrible at worst. In fact, I just finished reading a student's paper that had every one of the following errors on every single page. If that paper were an essay for a potential job offering, it would be completely unacceptable. Here are the top contenders for the worst errors:

1. **Misused words.** There are some commonly misused words that send up red flags and say to whoever is reading your essay that you haven't spent the time to learn the differences. Here are the most obvious:

    Affect: a verb that means to influence. "Rain will *affect* the baseball game."
    Effect: a noun that means the result. "Leaving the country had an *effect* on him."

    Accept: a verb meaning to receive. "He will *accept* the award this evening."
    Except: to leave out. "We packed everything in the car except for the luggage."

    Its: a possessive. "The group has *its* own clubhouse for meetings."
    It's: the contraction of "it is." "*It's* raining nonstop this morning."

    Farther: refers to distance. "I can throw *farther* than you can."
    Further: to a greater degree. "Let's go one step *further* and give the kitchen a second coat of paint."

    Loose: opposite of tight. "After dieting, my clothes are fairly *loose*."
    Lose: fail to win. "If we don't get some hits, we're going to *lose* this game."

    Principal: the head of a school or a sum of money. "Miss Smith is the *principal* of our school."
    Principle: a basic truth or law. "Honesty is the basic *principle* that guides us."

    Then: an adverb indicating time. "First we had dinner and *then* we went to the theater.

Than: a conjunction used for comparison. "He can pitch faster *than* anyone on the team."

Their: belonging to. "It is *their* debate to lose."
There: location of something. "Just put the food right over *there.*"
They're: contraction of "they are." "*They're* going on vacation to Europe for two weeks"

To: a preposition. "I'm going *to* the movies."
Too: means also or in excess. "She's going to the movies *too.*"

Whose: belonging to. "*Whose* pen is that?
Who's: the contraction for who is or who has." *Who's* going to class this morning?"

Your: a possessive. "Is this *your* car?"
You're: the contraction of "you are." "*You're* the funniest person I have ever known."

2. **Pronoun-antecedent disagreement.** This is a fairly common mistake students make. Whenever a sentence contains a singular subject, use *his* or *her*; whenever there's a plural subject, use *their*. An example is when writing the sentence "Each of us has to write their own paper." The sentence should either be written "Each of us has to write *his or her* own paper" or "All students have to write *their* own papers."

3. **Parallel structure flaws.** When writing a list of things in a sentence, students often mix up parts of speech. This can be confusing to readers. As an example, here's a sentence with parallel structure flaws: "After graduating from college, Bill wanted to pay off his loans, a good job, and health benefits." The sentence seems disjointed. It should read "After graduating from college, Bill wanted to pay of his loans, *get* a good job, and *have* health benefits."

    Another common problem is not being consistent with verbs throughout a sentence. For example, here's an awkward sentence: "The storm was bringing a lot of rain, pelted cars with hail, and took roofs off houses." It should read "The storm was *bringing* a lot of rain, *pelting* cars with hail, and *taking* roofs off houses." Notice how all the verbs – bringing, pelting, and taking – are all consistent and make the sentence smoother?

4. **Run-on sentences.** Sentences that are long are not necessarily run-ons. In fact, I've read a novel that had a sentence as long as the entire page. Run-on sentences are sentences that lack punctuation or words that connect thoughts. An easy way to fix them is simply to add commas, semicolons, periods, or words. Here are two examples and how to fix them:

Run-on: Once I finished showering, I left the house this morning I had eggs for breakfast.
Fixed: Once I finished showering, I left the house this morning after I had eggs for breakfast.

Run-on: Tracy ran out of the house without eating however she stopped on her way to work for a cup of coffee and biscuits she was so hungry.
Fixed: Tracy ran out of the house without eating. However, she stopped on her way to work for a cup of coffee and biscuits because she was so hungry.

5. **Spelling errors.** With today's word processing programs, there's really no excuse for spelling errors. Once you've written a paper, proofread it. If you're using a word processing program like Microsoft Word, most spelling errors and incorrect grammar will be underlined. If you have too many errors in your paper, you'll be seen as careless and lazy.

Punctuation Made Simple

Very often, the difference between a poorly written paper and a good one is the proper use of punctuation. A well-positioned comma or a semicolon can make a difference in how clear and concise a sentence is. Here are the most common punctuation rules to follow:

Commas

1. Use a comma after an introductory preposition phrase. "Starting with a good breakfast, John was ready for work."

2. Use commas to set off words. "Stars, as you know, are billions of miles away."

3. Use a comma to separate words that give added meaning. "A really fast runner, Bill won the race easily."

4. Use commas to separate items in a series. "The recipe called for milk, butter, eggs, and a pinch of salt."

5. Use a comma to separate parts of a compound sentence. "He drove his car to the store, and he later stopped at the restaurant to have lunch with his wife."

6. Use a comma after words that introduce a sentence. "Yes, I thought the exam was difficult."

7. Use a comma as a substitute for and, if it doesn't alter the meaning. "She admired his strong, masculine presence."

8. Use a comma to set off direct quotations. Alice asked, "Why aren't we going to the party?" or "Either ask her," Alice demanded, "Or just keep quiet about it."

One good rule of thumb is to use commas whenever it prevents confusion and misleading. Sometimes you can tell when you need a comma by reading something out loud and listening for a natural pause. For example, the sentence "To get over a bridge must be built" should be written "To get over, a bridge must be built."

Semicolons

1. Use a semicolon to separate clauses of compound sentences that do not have conjunctions such as and. "Ask not what your country can do for you; ask what you can do for your country."

2. Use a semicolon to separate sentences joined by the words however, nonetheless, or hence. "We tried to drive to the store; however, the snow was too deep." "Mary studied as hard as she could; nonetheless, she still got a C on the exam." "John spared no expense; hence he spent a lot of money."

3. Use semicolons for a more dramatic effect or a long pause. "I'm sorry to say that this will be my last day; and my last day will be a sad one indeed.

The Colon

1. Use a colon to introduce words and phrases or to summarize. "There are three main sections of a book: the introduction, the body, and the summary."

2. Use a colon to introduce a long quotation. "In his Gettysburg Address, Abraham Lincoln wrote: "Four score and seven years ago our fathers brought forth on this continent a new nation, conceived in Liberty, and dedicated to the proposition that all men are created equal."

3. Use a colon to introduce a list. "Before the semester begins, I need the following: pens, pencils, notebooks, and textbooks."

4. Use a colon to explain what was just written. "Death is a part of life: it is the culmination of our existence."

The Dash

1. Use a dash to set apart an explanatory or emphatic phrase. "The 4 main biomolecules – carbohydrates, proteins, lipids, and nucleic acids – are all essential for life."

2. Use a dash when there is a sudden break in the continuity of a sentence. "Let me tell you – and I will tell you – that you're not going to the party."

3. Use a dash to set off a summarizing phrase. "The critical factor in losing weight is how many calories you consume – that is the amount of certain foods that you eat."

Parentheses

1. Use parenthesis to set apart material not critical to a sentence and would not its meaning. "Every hour (same say less) the bell rings."

2. Use parentheses to enclose an abbreviation. "Diabetes mellitus (DM) affects some 20 million people in the United States."

3. Use parentheses to enclose numbers in a list. "Today we are (1) going to the mall, (2) dropping some letters off, and (3) having dinner with our parents."

Quotation Marks

1. Use quotation marks to enclose direct quotes. "What is the capital of Michigan?" he asked. "Please rise," the bailiff said as the judge entered the courtroom.

2. Use quotation marks to enclose words or phrases used in a special way. She is known by her friends as "the Party Animal" because of her penchant for going to every social gathering.

3. Commas and periods go inside quotation marks. "Get out of the building," ordered the fire marshal, "Before you get hurt."

Proofing and Editing Your Writing

Even good writers who know all about grammar and sentence structure make mistakes. That's where proof reading comes in. So once the writing is done, put it aside for a few days and then go back with fresh eyes. Never proof a manuscript you just wrote as soon as it's finished because you're just too familiar with it. Give the words some time to get out of your head; and when you come back to them, mistakes will literally jump out at you. There's a saying: you proof read with your eyes, you edit with your ears. Here are some suggestions for proofing and editing:

General tips for Proofing

- **Wait a few days before proofing anything.** Waiting a few days will erase what you have in your brain and force you to start fresh. You'd be amazed at how reading something 48 hours later makes sentences seem disjointed and ideas illogical. By seeing your words with a clear mind, you'll pick up even small errors more quickly.

- **Proof first thing in the morning.** Doing your proofreading before anything else clutters your mind is a good rule to follow. Many authors write during midday or evening and then sleep on it. They then begin the process of writing something new by proofing what they wrote the day before. This is also a great way to prevent writer's block.

- **Don't use fluorescent lighting.** Research has shown that fluorescent lighting interferes with accuracy. So if you want to pick up more errors and inconsistencies, proof next to a lamp with an incandescent bulb.

- **Read slowly.** This is not the time for speed reading and glossing over sentences. Slow down and you'll catch more errors.

- **Read out loud.** Reading aloud does two things: it forces you to slow down, which helps you pick up more errors, and it makes the mistakes and awkward sentences really stand out when you hear them. This is especially true when you've waited a few days before reading.

- **Proof in teams.** One trick that editors use is to work in teams that will read two copies of the manuscript. One person reads out loud while the other follows along. This method ensures that no one misses anything.

- **Proof your headings and subheadings.** Don't neglect these just because they're not part of the text. Headings are notorious for having errors because readers tend not to focus on them.

- **Be careful with small words.** It's common to write "it" or "in" when you mean "is" or "of" when you mean "if." These are usually caught when you read slowly and out loud.

- **Begin at the end.** If you're looking specifically for spelling or word errors and not for content errors, read one sentence at a time, starting with the last sentence and working your way back to the first one. This may seem like an odd way to read, but it prevents your brain from seeing what it expects to see.

Editing for Content and Style

- **Cut more than you add.** There's a saying in editing circles that "less is more." In almost every case, it's better to edit out unnecessary words than to insert more. Your writing will often flow better, be clear, and be more concise. Many students are too wordy because that's what they think good writing is all about. But every word needs to be there for a reason and not just to fill up the paper. If a word is unnecessary, be critical and get rid of it.

- **Skip the pretentious wording.** Eliminate words that are there just to impress. In other words, avoid the academic jargon and use words that everyone with at least an eighth grade education can understand. In reality, jargon excludes rather than includes most readers.

- **Use active versus passive voice.** Using the passive voice is a very weak and ineffective way to get a point across. For example, which of these sentences sounds better and conveys action more? "My car was driven to the next town," or "I drove my car to the next town." The first one suggests what happened while the second one tells exactly what happened. So to avoid the passive voice, avoid words like was, were, are, or am.

- **Avoid unnecessary adverbs.** Sometimes adverbs are needed; other times they are inappropriate and sometimes ridiculous. For example, in the sentence "He watched as the race car bolted past him quickly," why would you add the word quickly? Isn't it assumed that a race car that's bolting past you is quick? Why not just write, "He watched as the race car bolted past him." These kinds of needless adverbs can detract from an otherwise good paper.

- **Pay attention to math.** In many cases, students concentrate so much on trying to improve grammar, sentence structure, and punctuation that they ignore numbers. When proofing, scrutinize numbers, formulas, and calculations for any errors.

Being a good proof reader and a good editor takes patience. Many famous writers are terrible editors, which is why they rely so much on someone else doing their editing. It's a talent that a lot of people don't have but one that you can develop through practice. Follow the suggestions I've given you and you'll be a much better writer in no time at all.

Keys to Writing a Good Paper

It's something a lot of students dread on their first day of class: the announcement that there will be a midterm or final paper. In fact, they're so fearful that they avoid starting it until it's too late. It needn't be this way. Writing a paper can be stress-free and fairly easy if you follow these five basic steps:

1. **Organize the main ideas.** Begin your paper by writing an outline that maps out what you're going to write about. Jot down the main ideas and below those any material that will enhance and support the main ideas.

2. **Know what you're going to write about.** If you're assigned a specific topic, do some research. Use the internet, the library, or whatever you can to become familiar with the topic. If you're asked to write about your own topic, ask yourself what you're interested in and if there's something specific about the topic that you can uncover. Focus on specifics rather than generalities. For example, if you're asked to write a paper on hurricanes, spend a little time on hurricanes in general, how they form, etc., but focus more narrowly on a recent hurricane and write about it specifically.

3. **Write the first draft.** Every paper consists of an Introduction, which tells the reader what the main point is, the Body, which includes a number of paragraphs and examples that detail your main points, and a Conclusion, which summarizes your main ideas. In order to make your writing flow and be more interesting, use transition words and phrases at the beginning of paragraphs such as: however, nevertheless, moreover, for example, in addition, as a result, despite that, etc. Look for any repetitions throughout the paper as well.

4. **Proofread, edit, and write the final draft.** After a few days, use the previous suggestions to proof and edit your paper. Revise, reword, and refine your writing. Always read your paper slowly and out loud so that you'll notice any errors immediately. Then revise, revise, and revise again. Write your final draft and set it aside.

5. **Proofread and edit the final draft.** Once again, look for errors in punctuation, grammar, spelling, capitalization, etc. and keep an eye out for any inconsistencies. Also, look for awkward sentence structure, wordiness, and too much jargon.

Some Final Tips to Improve Writing

Writing to communicate is vital; and to be a good writer you need to use all the tools at your disposable in order to make sure that every one of your readers understands what you're trying to say. Knowing your audience and identifying your main ideas are the two most important rules to follow. Here are some final suggestions on how to make your writing really stand out:

- **Grab the reader's attention right away.** Well-crafted books hook you from page one and make you want to keep reading. That should be your goal; to place the most important idea in the first paragraph so that the reader focuses on it immediately. Once they know what you want to tell them, they'll keep reading.

- **Use the first line of each paragraph for your main idea.** Put your main message in the first sentence and then use the rest of the paragraph to expound on it.

- **Avoid capital letters.** If you want to emphasize, don't do it with capital letters. Use bold print or bullets instead. Besides making the reader feel like YOU'RE YELLING, capital letters are harder to read.

- **Mix short and long sentences.** Don't bore your readers by writing sentences that are always the same length. Add some variety. Follow a ten or twenty word sentence with a five or six word sentence. Here's an example: In a recent study, scientists had found that people who walked at least thirty minutes a day decreased their risk for developing type 2 diabetes. There was more to the study, however. The researchers also discovered that the receptors binding insulin actually increased several fold as the individuals increased the amount of walking they did each day. Some researchers disagreed. They . . . .

- **Be specific by using examples.** A good example can really clarify an idea. The following are two sentences. The first one is vague, the second is much better.

  Vague: Using a larger F-stop makes taking pictures in low light better.

  Better: Using a larger F-stop makes taking pictures in low light better because the aperture of the lens becomes larger and allows more light to enter the camera.

- **Leave enough white space.** Single spacing is much harder to read. Most teachers will ask that you double space because it's easier on the eyes. If they leave it up to you, make sure you double space.

- **Use bulleted lists.** Using bullets makes information easier to follow. Here are two examples. One is a long sentence; the other is effective.

Original: There are many ways to do strength training exercises, such as lifting free weights, using gym machines, and performing body weight exercises.

Better: Individuals can do strength training exercises various ways:

- lifting free weights
- using gym machines
- Performing bodyweight exercises

If you follow the suggestions in this chapter, you'll be well on your way to becoming a much better writer. Today, more than ever, you have to know how to communicate your point clearly and concisely. Together with reading skills, writing will determine your success in school. So the more you write and edit, the better your writing and editing will become and the better your grades will be.

6

Test-Taking Skills & Strategies

"The human spirit is never finished when it is
defeated; it is finished when it surrenders."
- Ben Stein, b. 1944

As a teacher for over 25 years, I've had students in my classes who should have been getting A's and B's but failed simply because they didn't know how to prepare for and take tests. I've also seen average students do much better than I thought they could because they learned what it takes to do well on certain types of exams. In many cases, getting good grades on tests is also a matter of knowing how to read questions.

There's really no secret to doing well on tests. All it takes is preparation and strategy. By the end of this chapter, you'll be able to do well on any kind of exam. And by using the tips and techniques for eliminating wrong choices, you'll increase your odds of getting correct answers.

Preparing For Tests

The first step in doing well on tests is to be prepared. This happens from day one of class by paying attention, taking good notes, keeping up with homework, and using effective study and review techniques. But once you begin to study in earnest for an exam, there are certain things you need to do in order to make your test preparation as good as it can be. Here are some suggestions:

- **Manage your time.** I'm sure you've heard it a thousand times but I'll say it for you again. Don't cram for exams! Instead, organize and budget your time and be studying and reviewing all along. Cramming may work on occasion and for some students, but for most it's not very effective at all.

- **Use review sessions.** At our school, we found that students who attend regular review sessions, even if they don't need to, typically do much better on exams than they would otherwise. They also end up getting much better final grades. Instructors at review sessions will often go over material that will be on their exams and give specific examples of questions that students will expect to see.

- **Practice the material.** Use practice tests, sample problems in the text or in your notes, review materials, and whatever else you can find, to learn the material. Recall the Power Law of Human Performance from chapter one: the time it takes an individual to perform a task decreases as the number of times the individual practices that task increases. In other words, your grade will reflect the amount of time you put into your study.

- **Make a review sheet.** Condense the exam material down to a single sheet with only the main ideas and key concepts. Use this as a guide that you can refer to several times when studying.

- **Get a good night's sleep.** All-nighters are a bad idea if you want to do well on an exam, especially if the exam is first thing in the morning. To get a good night's sleep, don't drink alcohol the evening before an exam, and don't eat a heavy meal at least 3 hours before going to bed.

- **Don't go to an exam hungry.** Nothing is worse than a growling stomach and hunger pangs in the middle of a test. So before your exam, eat a good meal that consists of protein and complex carbs. Avoid simple sugars, which cause an insulin spike, and heavy foods that will make you groggy.

- **Arrive 10 minutes early.** By getting to your exam a little early, you can relax and get yourself mentally prepared. Besides, if you arrive late you might miss any hints or last minute exam instructions.

- **Arrive prepared.** Always bring extra pens and pencils, erasers, a watch to pace yourself, and a calculator with fresh batteries.

- **Use the bathroom before an exam.** You don't want to be worrying about bodily functions while trying to concentrate on an exam. So go to the bathroom right before you go in to take your exam.

- **Prioritize the exam questions.** Once you get the exam, make a quick survey and answer the questions with the highest point values first. Do the ones you're most certain of, and don't spend time on a question you're stuck on, especially when you're pressed for time. You can always go back. In some cases, other parts of the test will have information that can trigger your memory and help you with a question you couldn't answer.

Multiple Choice Questions

Multiple choice tests are probably the most common tests that teachers give, especially in large classes. Students either like them or they don't; and some students are much better at answering multiple choice questions because they know the rules. The following are some tips for taking different types of multiple choice tests and doing well, even if you're not sure of the answer.

- **Answer the question before looking at the choices.** This strategy is effective if you know the material well. By answering the question and then looking at the multiple choice answers, you'll know that you're correct if you see your answer as one of the choices. Sometimes students get confused when answers seem similar, and this technique can eliminate that.

- **Eliminate wrong answers.** Sometimes you just know when an answer is wrong. By eliminating at least two wrong answers, you'll increase the odds that you'll get the correct answer just by guessing. One out of three is much better odds than one out of five.

- **Eliminate extremes.** In math and science courses, usually the correct answer is somewhere in the middle. For example, a biology exam might have the question "What is the pH of blood?" If the answers are a) 2.0 b) 4.5 c) 6.2 d) 7.4 e) 9.0, eliminate the extremes of 2.0 and 9.0 if you don't know and choose from the other three. The answer is 7.4.

- **Eliminate answers with absolutes.** Most answers are wrong if they contain all inclusive words like always, never, entirely, at no time, absolutely, etc. If you have to guess, choose from answers that contain qualifying words such as generally, usually, typically, for the most part, etc.

- **Eliminate choices with little information.** If you have to guess between an answer that has much information versus one that has little, choose the one with the most information. A long alternative is usually more correct than a short one.

- **Eliminate the more specific alternative.** When choosing between a general answer and a more specific one, usually the more general alternative is the correct answer.

- **Choose an opposite option.** When two totally opposite answers are given, one of those is likely to be correct. In that case, eliminate all other answers and choose between the two opposites.

- **Don't be fooled by "all of the above."** Here are the rules for dealing with *all of the above* and *none of the above* answers: if at least one of the answers is true, then eliminate the answer "none of the above." If at least two of the answers are true then the answer has to be "all of the above."

- **Don't change answers.** Students are notorious for changing answers they're not sure of. Usually your first choice is the correct one, so unless you're absolutely certain that you made a mistake the first time, don't change your answer.

- **Look for grammatical correctness.** Teachers are usually good at writing questions and answers that are grammatically correct. So if a question asks for a singular answer, don't choose the plural. For example, serine is "an" Amino Acid, not "an" carbohydrate.

True-False Questions

As easy as they may seem, true-false questions can really be tricky, especially if they're part of a standardized exam. One of the reasons is that teachers who write true-false questions like to include traps for students who don't pay attention to details. It's not that they want to be mean to students; it's that they want to make sure that students know the material. To answer these types of questions, you need to be on the alert for those traps. Here are some suggestions:

- **Watch for extreme qualifiers.** One word can make the difference between a true and false statement. What we call "all or none" words usually indicate a false answer and may include: all, always, entirely, every, invariably, never, and none. On the other hand, true statements typically include words like generally, ordinarily, usually, and for the most part.

- **Look for partial false statements.** If any part of a question or statement is false, then the entire statement has to be false. For example, in the statement *"The human body consists of more than 100,000 miles of blood vessels, all of them bringing oxygenated blood to cells, tissues and organs."* This statement may seem true at first but it's not, since some blood vessels like veins bring deoxygenated blood back to the heart. Another clue was the extreme phrase "all of them," which was a qualifier.

- **Watch for negative words.** These can change the entire meaning of a statement. Here are two examples:

  True: It is *characteristic* for politicians on to be talkative.

  False: It is *uncharacteristic* for politicians to be talkative.

  Also, watch out for double negatives that could change the meaning of a statement. So when you see a phrase such as *not unlikely*, scratch it out and make it into *likely*.

- **Guess true if you're not sure.** In most cases, a true-false exam will contains mostly true answers, so you'll have a better chance of getting it right. Of course, some teachers know this and might make most answers false, but that's usually not the case.

Short Answer Questions

The two keys to answering short answer questions are quickness and clarity. You have to organize your thoughts fairly rapidly, be able to put them in writing, and give explanations and examples in order to clarify what you're trying to say. Most short answer questions are graded on the overall quality of the response and the completeness of the answer. This is why knowing the material really well is going to help you formulate the answer quickly in your mind. The following are some tips for answering these types of questions in the best way possible:

- **Read the question carefully.** In some cases, short answer questions have several parts. Make sure you read and, if you have to, reread the question so that you understand what you're being asked. When you finish answering the question, go back and check to see if you left anything out.

- **Begin with a topic sentence.** You can either restate part of the sentence that you will use to address the question or statement, or begin with a key point that will address the rest of your answer. Here's an example:

Question: During cell division, describe the main differences between mitosis and meiosis.

Opening sentence: Mitosis and meiosis differ mainly in that mitosis involves cell duplication while in meiosis there is a reduction in the number of chromosomes.

- **Be concise.** By definition, short answers are brief and to the point. There shouldn't be any extra wording that will take away from the main point. So organize your thoughts, don't ramble or use very long sentences, and be specific and detailed. With these types of answers, longer is not always better.

- **Use examples.** When tackling a short answer question, it helps to include an example to illustrate your point. After introducing the key point in your opening sentence and then discussing it, you might add a sentence that begins with *For example, during mitosis the chromosomes . . .*

- **Never skip a question.** First of all, if you don't know the answer, go on to another question. Even when you're working on another answer, you'll be processing the previous question in your brain and you will eventually recall the information. Secondly, even if you don't, the physical act of writing something, even if it's only a few thoughts, will trigger your memory. Besides, there's always partial credit, and most teachers will give you something.

Essay Questions

With emails and texting so common today, many students have a difficult time with essay questions. Their grammar and sentence structure is poor, and they have trouble organizing their thoughts. They spend so much time using slang and abbreviations that when it comes to writing a clear, concise, and thoughtful essay, they're at a loss. If you're one of those students, you're going to be at a real disadvantage.

Essay questions can actually be easier than multiple choice or true-false questions because you have more time to think about the material and answer them, you can include more information, examples, and illustrations, and once you begin writing, your brain will take over and help you sort through the material you've learned. Here are some strategies for answering essay questions:

- **Stop for a moment and think.** If you've studied the material well, you know that it's in your brain. Sometimes closing your eyes and taking a brief pause to think about the question will jar your memory and give you the confidence to start writing.

- **Highlight the key points.** To make sure you understand the question, read it carefully and underline the main point of the question. If the question asks you to address several points, underline each of them so that you don't miss any.

- **Make a brief outline.** Like most students, you probably skip over this step because you think it's a waste of time. In fact, by making a quick outline with key points that you're going to address, you'll be better prepared to answer the question and you won't forget to include important information. You'll also be better organized and able to write in a clear and concise manner.

- **Organize your paragraphs.** Write a short introduction and then concentrate on the body of your essay. At the end, write a brief conclusion. To maintain clarity, focus on only one key idea in each paragraph, and edit your work when you're done. Don't include opinions unless the question asks for it, and never add irrelevant or extra information just to make your essay longer. That never works.

- **Always include examples and evidence.** This is even more important when answering essay questions than when answering short answer questions. If your class lecture notes include examples, use those. If not, come up with your own. Examples are a great way to show that you understand the concepts; and as a teacher I'm always impressed when students use good examples to illustrate key points.

- **Use essay key words to answer a question.** Key words are critical in answering an essay question and getting the most points possible. I can't tell you how many times I've had to take points off a question because a student, who knew the material, did not answer the question like I wanted it answered. Here are the most important keywords to look out for:

  Compare and contrast: To compare is to explain similarities; to contrast is to explain the differences. When a question asks you to compare and contrast something, explain how they are similar or different, don't just write a list of their similarities and differences. To prevent doing that, give examples.

  Describe or Discuss: When asked to describe or discuss something, you need to be more detailed and provide a thoughtful explanation. This is not simply a list of facts. For example, when asked to describe the characteristics of mammals, don't just list the characteristics like hair or fur, mammary glands, etc. Describe what fur does and give examples of mammals that survive cold because of fur. Describe how mammary glands function and why they're important to survival.

  Interpret: To interpret means to explain something from a graph, chart, figure, or illustration in your own words. Look at the data and think about it for a minute. Once you've analyzed it, explain what you see in writing.

List: When an essay question asks you to include a list, make sure that you explain beforehand what the list is. As an example, an essay question might ask you to describe the concept of global warming and list the factors that may be causing it. In this case, spend some time describing what global warming actually is and then list the factors that may be contributing to it.

Diagram or illustrate: This one is simple and straightforward. When asked to include a diagram, make a drawing and label it. Don't assume that the instructor will figure out what you've drawn or that he/she assumes you know what you're drawing. Labels indicate that you know the material.

- **Be neat and use proper grammar.** Even though most instructors won't take off for sloppiness and poor grammar, unless it's an English exam, they may not look at your answer as favorably. However, with the emphasis on reading and writing skills these days, many instructors will take off for grammar. If you want as many points as possible, be neat and construct your sentences in a way that make sense. After all, it doesn't matter if you know the material if you can't explain it in a way that is readable. So go back and reread the rules for grammar, punctuation, and sentence structure in chapter 5. There's nothing more frustrating than trying to figure out how to write something when the clock is running.

Oral Exams

Of all exams given, this one has to be the most hated. Most of us feel much more comfortable when we're not put on the spot and expected to answer a question with the instructor staring directly at us. Moreover, oral exams can be open-ended, with the instructor continuing to ask you questions based on answers you give to previous questions. But oral exams don't have to be as bad as you think if you prepare as well as you would for any other exam. The following tips will help you get through any oral exam with skill and confidence:

- **Know the rules and the topics.** Never go into an oral exam not knowing how it will be presented or not knowing what topic areas will be covered. The best way to do this is by getting to know an instructor and asking him/her for information before the exam. If you've never talked to your instructor, you won't be very comfortable in the exam. Once you know what the topics will be, make yourself an outline and then write down some questions you think you might be asked.

- **Practice for the exam.** Just studying the material is not enough to ensure a good grade. You have to be prepared to discuss the topic by practicing either by yourself in front of a mirror or with fellow students who will ask you questions. The more you practice, the more confident you'll be when you finally have to take the exam.

- **Dress appropriately.** While you don't have to come to the exam in your Sunday finest, show a little respect for the instructor by dressing conservatively. That means no flip flops, no pants hanging down, no tee shirts, and no shorts.

- **Be polite.** As soon as you get to the exam, introduce yourself and maintain eye contact. Listen carefully to what the instructor is saying and repeat it if necessary so that you understand exactly what you're being asked. Never interrupt a question; wait until the instructor is finished before asking for clarification. And make sure you turn off your cell phone before walking in the door.

- **Organize your thoughts.** Don't answer a question immediately. Give it some thought so that you can gather yourself and think of the correct answer. When you begin, get to the point and use complete and concise sentences. Once you're finished, ask the instructor if there's anything else he/she would like you to add in case you left something out.

- **End on a positive note.** When the exam is finished, don't just get up and leave. Smile, thank the instructor, and tell him/her that you are enjoying the class so far. Ending on a pleasant note leaves a good impression; and even though you're not supposed to get extra points for being a nice student, it can't hurt.

How to Take a Math Exam

For many students, math is their hardest subject because they are learning a new language consisting of numbers and constantly expanding formulas. They find that they need to study more for math than for any of their other classes; and if they fall behind in math topics it's hard to catch up because math concepts and principles build on one another. Probably no other subject requires that you know one concept before going on to the next.

Taking math exams is no different than taking any other exam in that you need to be studying all along and not cramming the night before. However, being good at math requires a lot of practice working a variety of problems because you'll be tested on skill rather than on memorization. And just like anything else, to get good at a particular skill, you need to practice that skill over and over. The following are some effective strategies for developing those skills and doing well on math exams:

Before the Exam

- **Do homework.** Math requires practice and repetition; and there's no way that you'll do well on exams if you don't work problems outside of class. Use your textbook to work extra problems. Instructors often use homework assignments to make up exam questions, and it's nice to see a problem almost identical to one that you've already worked out.

- **Make a crib sheet.** On a single sheet of paper, write down important formulas. Review the sheet every time you study and work homework problems. Before the exam, go over your crib sheet one final time and make sure that you've memorized all the important formulas.

- **Ask questions.** Don't move on to the next concept until you're sure that you understand the last one. Remember, math principles build on each other, so go to review sessions and ask your instructor to explain what you don't understand.

- **Learn to do word problems.** Word problems make students panic like no other math problem does. These can be made a lot easier if you've studied the material really well and can use the concepts you've learned to solve the problems. No matter what kind of word problem you're asked to solve, there are certain rules to follow. They are:

  1. *Read the question twice.* Most students make the mistake of reading a question quickly and then starting to answer it right away. What to do instead is read the question once to get an idea of what the problem is about and then reread it to make sure that you understand exactly what you're being asked to do.

2. ***Write down the variables.*** Choose letters for your known and unknown variables. For example, if the question tells you that a known radius is 15, write: R = 15. If a question gives you an unknown variable you need to find such as the area of a room, write: Let A = area of the room.

3. ***Make a drawing.*** After reading and rereading, it may help to draw a figure or a table that you can label. Drawings can add clarity and make a problem more understandable. You might even get partial credit if the instructor sees that you were on the right track.

4. ***Translate key words.*** One of the biggest stumbling blocks in doing word problems is figuring out the equation to use in order to solve the problem. So to do well on a word problem, you must translate English into the language of mathematics. The following table illustrates how key words are used.

Key Words	Mathematical Operations
increased by, total of, sum total, together, more than, combined	Addition
decreased by, less than, minus, difference of, fewer than	Subtraction
multiplied by, the product of, times, of	Multiplication
Per, ratio of, quotient of, percent of, out of	Division
Yields, was, were, is, are, was, were, gives	Equal

During the Exam

• **Write down key formulas.** Unless your instructor allows you to bring a crib sheet to the exam, write down key formulas in the margins or on the back of the exam before you even look at the questions. This will guarantee that you have your formulas handy before the stress of the exam causes you to freeze up.

- **Work the easiest problems first.** Take a quick survey of the exam and pick out the easiest problems. Doing these first will ensure that you have enough time to work on harder problems later. It will also ease your anxiety and help build confidence. If you find yourself spending too much time on a single question, skip it and go back to it at the end.

- **Work neatly.** Careless mistakes translate into lost points; so be neat and show all your work in an clean and orderly manner. Instructors will give partial credit if you got a wrong answer but have written down all the steps. If all you did was make a minor addition or subtraction error, or misplaced a decimal, you'll probably get most of the points anyway.

- **Go back over your work.** At the end of the exam, go back over your work and correct any mistakes or omissions. If you're not sure of your initial answer but can't decide if another answer is more correct, then leave it alone. Unless you're absolutely certain about your correction, the first answer is usually the right one. Besides, students who spend a lot of time dwelling on a question can actually talk themselves into a wrong answer.

Open Book Exams

In some cases, an open book exam can be more difficult than a closed book exam since an instructor knows that you'll have access to the course material and, therefore, will make it harder. To do well on these types of exams, you have to be very familiar with the textbook so that you know exactly where to turn for the information you need. Focus mainly on principles, key concepts and main ideas, and mark those pages with post-it notes or other markers. It's a good idea to label the post-it notes in order to make searching easier.

Another helpful technique, if the instructor allows it, is to make a crib sheet with the important ideas written down in an organized way. And just as you would for other exams, answer the easiest questions first and then go back and finish the rest of the exam. If you've highlighted the main concepts in the book, they'll be easy to spot and use as quotes in your answer.

Reducing Test Anxiety

It's good to be concerned about an exam and your grades; it's not good to have text anxiety because that can interfere with your ability to do well on future exams. Students who suffer from text anxiety can be extremely self-critical and tend to worry constantly about how grades will affect their future. Instead of feeling challenged by the prospect of success, they become so afraid of failure that they become stressed at the very thought of taking an exam. When they do poorly, it makes them think that they're not the good student they thought they were. They often blame the teacher for their poor performance, which makes correcting the problem even more difficult.

One of the biggest problems with test anxiety is that it directs your attention away from the material you need to learn and away from productive ways to study. You become less organized and less effective in your study habits, which then leads to poor test scores and low grades. This can be very frustrating, especially if it keeps happening in all your courses. Overcoming text anxiety is simple, but it requires that you get in the habit of doing certain things. Here are some effective tips:

- **Space out study.** The worse thing to do is to wait until the last minute to study. By spreading out your study sessions over days or weeks and reviewing several times, you'll feel more prepared and decrease anxiety. The night before the exam, go over the material but don't cram. Rest, exercise, eat well, and get a good night's sleep.

- **Maintain a regular routine during exam week.** Nothing is more disruptive to good study habits and effective learning than starting something new during exam week. So maintain your focus and concentrate on learning rather than on something that will take your mind off schoolwork.

- **Avoid negative students.** Panic and negativism are contagious and are spread to even the best students. If someone is continually negative, it's time to make some new friends who have positive attitudes.

- **Come prepared.** Have a special exam kit that includes pens, pencils, erasers, paper, ruler, calculator, tissues, and, if allowed, a small snack you can quietly munch on.

- **Read directions carefully.** As soon as the test is handed out, read the directions. If there's something you don't understand, ask right away. Never wait until you're well into the exam before asking the instructor for clarification.

- **Write down important information immediately.** As soon as you get the exam, spend the first few minutes writing down formulas, ideas, facts, and key words in the margins or on the back of the exam. Do this before you see the questions and when your mind is still fresh. Then, when you start answering questions, refer to your notes. Having the information written down is a great way to ease the anxiety of trying to come up with answers on the spot.

- **Assess the questions.** Scan the test before you begin and see what types of questions are being asked (multiple choice, essay, matching, etc.) and the number of points they're worth. This way you'll know how to budget your time, which questions are worth the most points, and which ones you'll need to spend more time on.

- **Answer the easiest questions first.** This gets you off to a good start and helps build confidence for the remaining questions. Then, when you come to the remaining questions, don't get upset if you come across one you can't answer. Skip it and go on to the next. Your brain will subconsciously process that information and before long it will trigger your memory. If you dwell on questions you can't answer, you'll get flustered and you'll be wasting a lot of time not answering the questions you do know.

No matter how good a student you are, you're not going to know every answer on every exam. So instead of hoping that you're not going to bomb the test, tell yourself that you studied enough and that you are going to do well. The most important thing is to be well prepared and stay relaxed. If you've taken good notes, studied hard, and reviewed all along, you'll feel much better about your chances. And once you start doing well on exams, the positive reinforcement will feed on itself and you'll feel less and less anxious about taking exams.

7

Oral Presentations

"You must do the things you think you cannot do."
- Eleanor Roosevelt, 1884-1962

As a student, you'll most likely be taking classes that require you to give one or more oral presentations. Once you graduate, chances are that you'll be giving your fair share of oral presentations as well. In fact, the ability to speak well in front of people is one of the most sought after skills a person can have. It ranks right up there with reading and writing abilities, and it will give you a definite advantage over individuals who may be able to write well but who don't have good oral communication skills. In a recent business survey, employers looking to hire listed speaking ability as one of their top criteria for employment because it is now considered a "21st century skill."

Making a good oral presentation requires that you follow certain rules and guidelines. It takes practice; sometimes a lot of practice to be able to give a good presentation. An effective speaker should know his/her audience in order to decide how to make the presentation, prepares well, makes a good first impression, uses proper body language, and is well organized and confident. Before giving any oral presentation, it's important that you ask yourself these five basic questions:

1. Who is my audience?

2. How much do they already know?

3. What do I need to tell them to keep them interested?

4. What do I want them to learn about my topic?

5. What types of questions can I anticipate?

By asking these questions, you'll make sure that you prepare your presentation in a way that keeps the audience interested, engaged, alert, and informed. This will also help you in researching and planning the presentation. Some experts will tell you that oral communication can't be taught; and that unless you're a gifted speaker, it's a personal skill that requires a lot of practice. This chapter will help you become a better speaker regardless of your abilities and make oral presentations easier and more natural.

Things to Think About Beforehand

Before you give your oral presentation, there are things you need to do, sometimes several times, in order to make it the best it can be. By preparing beforehand, you'll be less apprehensive and nervous and you'll be confident in your ability to get the best grade you can. Here are some pre-presentation tips:

- **Practice, practice, practice.** No one gives a good oral presentation without spending some time practicing. And that doesn't mean reading over your index cards or looking at your PowerPoint slides and thinking that that's enough. For someone who hasn't given oral presentations before, it may take a lot of practice. And by practice I mean giving your oral presentation out loud as if you were actually presenting it to an audience.

- **Time yourself.** When my students give oral presentations, one of the reasons for their losing points is going over or under the time limit. That indicates to me that they didn't practice enough to know how long the presentation would take. If your instructor gives you 15 minutes, don't go for 10 minutes, and certainly don't go for 25 minutes. Add some material if it's too short, edit out if it's too long.

- **Practice in front of a mirror.** Looking at yourself while you give an oral presentation will help you catch any strange facial expressions or body movements that would be distracting to your audience. Smile like you would in front of an audience, and make eye contact with yourself as you would with other people.

- **Record yourself.** When you practice, record yourself and then listen carefully for mistakes. Listen for unusual pauses and excessive use of words like *and so*, *well*, *anyway*, *like*, etc. You may be so used to saying these words that it's second nature. When you hear them over and over on a recording, they'll jump out at you.

- **Make index cards.** Have index cards as a backup to your PowerPoint slides. Write clearly in large letters, double space, and number them in the order of your presentation just in case you drop them.

How to Organize an Oral Presentation

An oral presentation consists of three parts: an introduction, the body, and the conclusion. The introduction prepares the audience for what the topic is about and sets the stage for the rest of your talk. It gives an overview of what the audience is to expect. This is also a good time to include a joke, a story, or some interesting fact about the topic. The body is the main part of the presentation and should include examples, illustrations, charts, and other visual aids that will make your presentation clear and interesting. The conclusion summarizes the topic and reinforces the key points of your presentation.

When you're assigned an oral presentation, you need to prepare and plan by asking yourself a series of questions that will determine how you'll organize your talk. Using the following checklist is an easy way to make sure that you have everything you need and that your presentation will be as organized as possible.

Questions To Ask	Answers
Who is my target audience?	

What is the title of my presentation?	
What is the purpose of my presentation?	
What are the main points?	
Where is the presentation going to be?	
What time of day is the presentation?	
How long will my presentation last?	
Will I use PowerPoint or transparencies?	
What type of equipment do I need?	
Will the equipment be provided?	
Will I need a whiteboard?	
Is there a podium?	
How am I supposed to dress?	
Do I need handouts or other material?	

The Introduction

The beginning of your presentation is the most important part because you're setting the stage for everything else that follows. If you lose your audience at the start, it's difficult to get them back. So you have to establish a personal and professional connection with the audience and get their complete and undivided attention. You do this by following 4 rules:

1. **Greet your audience.** Begin your presentation by smiling and saying hello, good morning or good afternoon and then introduce yourself. *"Okay, let's get started. Good morning everyone. My name is John Smith and I'm going to talk to you this morning about . . ."*

2. **Introduce the topic.** As soon as you get everyone's attention and finish introducing yourself, outline exactly what your presentation is going to be about. Tell the audience approximately how long you'll be speaking and then draw them into the subject matter by either asking a question or bringing out an emotion. Here are two examples:

   "This morning I'd like to spend the next fifteen minutes talking about the effects of pollution on the decreased number of honey bees in the United States. Have you ever thought about the number of plants and crops that would become extinct if there were no bees to pollinate them?"

   "This morning I'd like to spend the next fifteen minutes talking about the effects of pollution on the decreased number of honey bees. I'm sure that some of you have heard about the massive loss of honey bees around the country and how it's affecting farmers."

3. **State your purpose.** After you introduce the topic and give the audience something to think about, tell them what the purpose of your presentation is. *"What I'd like to present this morning are the reasons for the sudden decline in the bee population and some techniques that scientists are using to reverse this decline and prevent future problems in the bee industry."*

4. **Outline your presentation.** The final part of your introduction is a brief 2 or 3 point outline that will tell the audience what they will expect to hear for the next 15 minutes or so. *"I've divided my presentation into 3 parts. In the first part, I'll explain what many scientists believe is the root cause of the declining bee population around the country. In the next part, I'll discuss the effects that this decline is having on the food supply. And in the last part, I'll describe techniques that scientists are using to bring our bee populations back to normal levels."*

The Body of a Presentation

The main part of a presentation is the body, where you discuss, explain, defend, and illustrate what you've just introduced. There should be no extra fluff here. Everything you say in this main section must support your purpose. You do this most effectively with examples, charts, photos, and diagrams. Like the introduction, there are rules you need to follow for the body of a presentation. They are:

1. **Organize your ideas.** Make a concise outline of your presentation and then organize it in a sequence that will maintain interest and keep the audience's attention.

2. **Limit the content.** If you only have a certain amount of time to give a presentation, you need to be concise. Don't ramble on with extra information just to impress your audience or fill up your allotted time. The quality of your material and your examples is more important than the quantity, so develop your topic carefully, use examples that are related to that topic, and focus in on the main ideas and concepts.

3. **Edit your slides.** Be careful about spelling, grammar, and punctuation. A poorly edited PowerPoint slide show can be distracting and take away from your presentation. Also, have some talking points to add.

4. **Keep it interesting.** Use unique examples and colorful illustrations. A picture is worth a thousand words, so don't neglect them. Also, use pleasing colors, but don't overdo it.

5. **Use attention grabbers.** Unless you're a very dynamic speaker, and the audience isn't really interested in the topic, you probably won't hold the audience's attention for more than 5 or 10 minutes. So, every 3 to 5 minutes throw in a slide with an interesting visual, tell a short story, or write something on the whiteboard or flip chart. If you do this every few minutes, you'll hold everyone's attention until the end of your presentation.

6. **Make transitions obvious.** Tell the audience when you're moving on from one part of your presentation to another.

7. **Use lists to make a point.** A list is a great ways to organize material and help the audience focus in on your topic. Here's an example:

Three techniques that scientists are using to bring our bee populations back to normal levels are:

1. *Developing new pesticides to fight bee fungal infections*
2. *Transplanting bee populations to affected areas*
3. *Creating new fungus-resistant species of bees*

The Conclusion

The conclusion is one of the most important parts because it summarizes in a few key sentences what you just spent fifteen or more minutes talking about. A good conclusion reminds the audience of what they are there to listen to and stimulates enough interest to ask questions. It should always include four parts:

1. **A brief summary of the main points.** In a few short sentences, remind the audience of the key ideas and important points of the presentation. *"As you've seen in this presentation, the main areas of concern are . . ."*

2. **Brief concluding remarks.** Following the list of main points and ideas, offer a personal opinion, some commentary, future research, lessons learned, and/or recommendations based on your findings. Make sure your audience knows that you're finishing. *"So, in conclusion, we've seen how . . ."*

3. **A sentence thanking the audience.** Always thank the audience for their attention and for being there. *"I'd like to thank you for being here this morning."*

4. **An invitation for questions.** Conclude the presentation by stepping away from the podium and asking for questions. *"I'd be happy to answer any questions you might have."*

Final Tips for Effective Presentations

To give a good presentation, you need to follow some basic rules and guidelines about your delivery style, speech, and voice quality, ability to create interest, body language, and use of visual aids. The following are five foolproof tips that will make your oral presentations stand out from the rest:

1. **Use clear and concise examples.** Every few slides, illustrate what you're saying with an appropriate example. Preface it by saying, *"To illustrate this . . ."* or *"As an example . . ."*

2. **Refer to what you've said and what you're going to say.** During the early part of the presentation, repeat what you've told the audience but in a different way. *"As we've already seen . . ."* Then entice them with what they will hear. *"A little later we'll see how . . ."*

3. **Use proper body language.** Body language includes movement, eye contact, facial expressions, and hand gestures. The best way to avoid negative body language is to breathe deeply for a few seconds before you speak, and stay calm and natural. Start the presentation by smiling, and avoid the following pitfalls:

   - Don't keep looking down at your notes or up on the screen; look around at the audience and make eye contact with everyone in the room, but don't stare too long at any one individual.

   - Don't slouch, sway back and forth, or keep your hands in your pockets.

   - Don't gesture wildly to make a point.

   - Don't turn your back to the audience.

   - Don't sit down or lean against the podium.

   - Don't pace across the room as you give your presentation.

   - Don't grimace or make unusual facial expressions.

4. **Speak clearly.** Some of the worst presentations I've seen were ones where the speakers spoke too fast or too slow or mumbled. When you practice the presentation in front of a mirror, see that you're opening your mouth and enunciating clearly. Listen for garbled words or words that run together. Here are some things to look out for:

   - Don't use a monotone voice. Change your pitch when emphasizing a key topic.

   - Don't start your sentences with fillers such as *"You know"* or *"Um."*

- Don't rush through your presentation. Sometimes if a speaker has too much material for the allotted time or is nervous, he/she will try to speed things up. You'll avoid this by preparing well and by practicing.

- Don't use language or technical jargon that your audience will not understand, especially if the material is complex. The last thing you want is for your audience to be thinking about how your speaking instead of what you're saying. Make sure you use proper grammar.

5. **Use effective visuals.** Visuals are graphs, charts, photos, drawings, and illustrations that help focus the audience's attention and make the presentation more interesting. The most common way to show these now is PowerPoint, but you may also use transparencies or overheads. Some rules to follow are:

- Unless you have a specific reason not to, make the layout horizontal, since it's easier to visualize that way.

- Use a normal font style such as Times Roman, Helvetica, Ariel, or Courier. The point size should be at least 30 for a major heading and 20 or 16 for the subheadings and text.

- Use a white or lighter shade background. This makes the text look clearer than a darker color background.

- Use color for graphics and black for text. However, avoid too many colors or too many different type faces.

- Use **bold face**, *italics*, and underlining to emphasize text, but don't overdo it. Too many capital letters, italics, or bold letters detract from the presentation.

- Limit the number of slides. There comes a point when too many slides will actually put the audience to sleep, no matter how interesting the subject matter might be. A slide every two minutes is about right.

- Use a pointer or a laser pointer to draw attention to a specific point on a slide.

- Don't just read from your slides or note cards. This never sounds natural, and the audience will assume that you haven't prepared. The best way to use note cards is to write down the main ideas and key points, and then use them as reminders of what you will say. This works well if you practice the presentation a few times beforehand.

6. **Dress appropriately.** Appearance is important, so don't overlook it. Whether you like it or not, your audience and your instructor will subconsciously judge you by the way you look. The best rule is to dress conservatively and be well groomed. That means no shorts, flip flops, tank tops, or tee shirts.

Sample Oral Presentation Outline

The following example is a simple template you can use for an oral presentation. The number of slides you'll use will depend on how many minutes your presentation will be. Depending on how much detail there is on a slide, you'll typically spend 1-2 minutes per slide.

Opening

Greet the audience and get everyone's attention.

Title and author (slide #1)

Effects of Pollution on Bee Populations by John Smith.

Introduction

State the topic, use an attention grabber, state your purpose, and outline what you'll be presenting

1. "This morning I'd like to talk about the effects of pollution on the decreased number of honey bees. I'm sure that some of you have heard about the massive loss of honey bees around the country and how it's affecting farmers."

2. "What I'd like to present this morning are the reasons for the sudden decline in the bee population and some techniques that scientists are using to reverse this decline and prevent future problems in the bee industry."

3. "I've divided my presentation into three parts. In the first part, I'll explain what scientists believe is the root cause of the declining bee population. In the next part, I'll discuss the effects that this decline is having on the food supply. And in the last part, I'll describe techniques that scientists are using to bring our bee populations back to normal levels."

Body of the presentation (slides #2 -10)

Begin discussing your main points by giving supporting evidence and using examples, diagrams, charts, figures, and illustrations.

I.   Root cause of declining bee population
   a.   Fact #1
   b.   Fact #2
   c.   Fact #3

II. Effects of decline on food supply
   a.   Fact #1
   b.   Fact #2
   c.   Fact #3

III. Techniques for bringing bee populations back to normal levels
   a.   Fact #1
   b.   Fact #2
   c.   Fact #3

Conclusion (slides 11-12)

Summarize the key points, offer a conclusion, and tell the audience what the future holds.

"In conclusion, bee populations have been on the decline . . ."

"Based on the research done so far, scientists believe that. . . ."

Backup slides (slides 13-15)

Have a few backup slides ready just in case you need to answer a specific question about something you may not have gone over in detail.

Final Checklist

The following is a sample evaluation form I use to grade oral presentations. The values are 1-5 with 1 being poor and 5 being excellent.

Student Name:					
Title of Presentation:					
Start Time:　　　　End Time:　　　　Total Elapsed Time:					
Category Checklist	**Grade**				
Appearance and Dress	1	2	3	4	5
Body Language	1	2	3	4	5
Eye Contact	1	2	3	4	5
Delivery Style and Effectiveness	2	4	6	8	10
Grammar	2	4	6	8	10
Vocabulary	1	2	3	4	5
Use of Visual Aids	2	4	6	8	10
Knowledge of Topic	2	4	6	8	10
Use of Appropriate Examples	2	4	6	8	10
Good Transition Between Slides	1	2	3	4	5
Summary of Main Points	1	2	3	4	5
Effective Conclusion	2	4	6	8	10
Question and Answer Session	1	2	3	4	5
Use of Allotted Time	1	2	3	4	5

8

Taking Online Courses

"Whether you think you can or think you can't, you are right."
-Henry Ford, 1863-1947

Online classes seem to be more popular than ever, especially for older students who have families or for individuals who have full time jobs or live far from campus. In response to this growing demand, colleges and universities are adding online courses at a record pace and in almost every field of study. But although online study is great for many people, not everyone has the discipline or the personality to be successful in an online class. There are also disadvantages that you need to be aware of before diving in and regretting it later.

Advantages

Flexibility: Online classes offer much more flexibility than having to show up at exactly the same time on exactly the same days of the week. You can do an assignment while eating lunch, taking a break while at work, or sitting under a tree in the park. There's no attendance other than having to log in and do your work whenever you want. This is great for individuals who have jobs and families.

Ease of Scheduling: You don't have to worry about time conflicts with other courses when registering for online classes. There's no such thing as lecture overlap, so you can fit in courses you might not have been able to fit in if you were taking regular classes.

Cost: Online and regular courses may have the same tuition rates, buy if you take into account your transportation costs and the fact that you probably will spend money for food while you're on campus, online classes can actually save you some money.

Disadvantages

Little interaction: Unlike regular classes, you won't be seeing your course instructor very much, if at all. In some cases, the only way to have any communication is by telephone or email. If you're the type of student who likes a lot of face time with teachers, online classes won't work well for you.

Require self-discipline: Many students need a bit of motivation from instructors because there's often no established routine. If you're not a self-starter, and you find it difficult to get going on assignments by yourself, you'll fall behind quickly and not be able to catch up.

Learning style may not fit: If you're a kinesthetic or auditory learner, online classes may not be a good fit for you, especially when there are no videos available or discussions with other students.

Online classes may not be accepted at other schools: Some online classes will not be accepted if you transfer to another school. Before taking an online class, make sure that it meets all the requirements necessary for your major and for transfer.

Requirements for Online Learning

Instructors of online classes assume that students registering for their class meet certain requirements. It's a given that you will need a good computer, or have ready access to one, know how to use it, and be familiar with the Internet and word processing programs like Microsoft Word. But you also need to know your strengths and weaknesses so that you can be successful. Ask yourself these questions before you start any online course:

1. Do I have a reliable computer with current anti-virus software, and a reliable printer?

2. Do I know how to create and upload files to my computer, send email attachments, and create PDF files?

3. Do I have a fast and reliable Internet connection?

4. Do I know how to do an effective Internet search?

5. Do I know how to use Blackboard or whatever learning platform the school is using for their online courses?

6. Do I read and write well, since any online course requires a good deal of reading and written communication?

7. Do I meet deadlines and try never to procrastinate?

8. Do I have the self-discipline to log in every day and do assignments, even when I have other things I'd rather be doing?

9. Do I prefer to learn alone or would I rather interact in a classroom setting with my peers?

10. Do I find it easy to telephone or email an instructor if I need help with a problem?

If you answered *"yes"* to most of the questions, then you won't run into any problems taking an online course. From my experience, the biggest issue is the freedom students have, which makes them feel as if they can put off studying and doing assignments because they can study and do their work any time they want. Don't make that mistake. Online classes can be as demanding, if not more demanding, than regular classes, so you need to stick to a routine and keep up.

Selecting Online Courses

Selecting an online class is based mainly on personal preference or convenience, but in some cases you might have time conflicts and would like to take an online course because it fits better into your schedule. Sometimes that's a mistake, especially if the course is difficult or if you feel that you would get a better grade if you took the same course in a regular class.

Every student is different; and only you know your strengths and limitations. But before you decide to take an online course in a specific subject, know that certain areas are more difficult than others. A 10-year study done at Wake Forest University showed that, based on GPA, some college degrees are more difficult than others. In other words, the more difficult the degree, the lower the GPA was, and the easier the degree, the higher the GPA.

The following are lists of the hardest and easiest college degrees based on grades and GPA. Of course schools vary in how difficult their courses are, but a national average of student GPAs shows that certain courses are harder than others. Unless you're a good student and very self-disciplined and dedicated, you may want to avoid taking those as online courses.

Hardest College Majors

1. Chemistry and Biochemistry
2. Mathematics
3. Economics
4. Psychology
5. Biology
6. Geology
7. Philosophy
8. Geography
9. Physics
10. Political Science

Easiest College Majors

1. Education
2. Languages
3. English
4. Music
5. Religion
6. Sociology and Anthropology
7. Art
8. History
9. Computer Science
10. Philosophy / Religious Studies

From my experience, the list is a little misleading in several ways. Computer science, for example, is on the easy list, but we all know that computer science classes can be really tough. The reason so many computer science majors have higher than average GPAs is because typically only very good students choose computer science as a major. I've also found that the reason many chemistry, math, biology, and physics majors have lower GPAs is because they're totally ill-prepared for those courses when they get into college. Some students, who thought they knew chemistry and math because they did well in high school, are shocked when they take these college-level courses and see how difficult they really are. In many cases, math is the principle obstacle to doing well in the physical science courses.

The bottom line is that you're the only one who can decide if you're ready to take an online course, particularly if it's one that's especially difficult for most students. If you're realistic, you know your abilities and, above all, you're honest with yourself about your maturity and time management skills, you should do as well in online classes as you would taking an in-class course. However, if you already have a grueling schedule and are in a tough major, think twice about adding an online class just because you can fit it in.

Online Course Guidelines

Once you've registered for an online class, don't wait until the class begins in order to start preparing, especially if you've never taken an online class before. Too many students wait until their first day and then find out that they can't access the system, they don't know how to navigate the pages, they can't find information, or they're not sure where to look for the syllabus, etc. The following are some tips to prevent stress and get you off to the right start:

- **Get yourself organized.** Because online classes require that you be motivated and self-disciplined, prepare a designated workspace that you know will always be available, make some folders to keep assignments and other materials in, and test your computer and printer to make sure that they're compatible with the school's online learning system. Check the school's distance learning center for specific requirements.

- **Ask questions.** If there's something you don't understand or can't find in the syllabus or textbook, don't be passive. Contact the instructor and ask for clarification. As an online instructor, one of my biggest pet peeves is students waiting until it's too late to ask for help. The day of an online exam is not the time to be asking your instructor how to access the test.

- **Get familiar with the course.** Long before the class even begins, print out and go over the syllabus, make sure you understand the course requirements and assignments, look through the textbook, and review the PowerPoint slides and other reading materials. Don't assume that once the course starts, the instructor will guide you every step of the way. He or she will assume that you're responsible enough to have gone through the course materials beforehand.

- **Set a schedule.** Some of my online students fall behind and miss due dates and assignments because it becomes very easy to procrastinate. To keep up with your work, print out the exam and assignment schedules and mark these down in a calendar or a schedule book. Set aside a specific time and day of the week that you will dedicate to online assignments. Just think of it as going to a regular class except that you'll be sitting at home in front of a computer.

- **Don't neglect discussion boards.** A good portion of your grade when taking an online class is discussions. Make sure you know the rules and requirements for participating in a discussion. When the instructor posts a question, answer it as completely as you can and also respond to other students' posts as well. Students who participate in discussion boards regularly and on time are viewed as interested and motivated, and will be rewarded accordingly. Always be polite, and never be critical of the instructor or another student.

- **Take an active interest.** If there's one way to impress an instructor and influence your grade other than test scores, it's showing how interested you are in the course. You do this by participating, asking questions, offering opinions, and corresponding with the instructor. Some effective ways to positively influence how an instructor sees you are:

Telling the instructor what you like about the course

Responding quickly to inquiries and suggestions

Turning in all your assignments on time

Thanking the instructor for any comments, critiques, or corrections

Not being argumentative or critical of how the course is being taught

Not being overbearing or too demanding

Admitting mistakes and acknowledging that you want to do well

Although it's unethical for an instructor to give extra points to a student for no reason, there's always wiggle room when giving points for essay and discussion questions. An instructor may tend to be more lenient or forgiving with a student he/she knows is truly interested in the course.

- **Participate in chat rooms.** Students often use chat rooms where they can get tips and suggestions from other students. This is especially helpful if other students have taken online courses before and are willing to help you. Sometimes chat rooms are used by the instructor so that everyone can participate at the same time.

Communicating and Online Courses

One of the biggest differences, and sometimes the greatest challenge, between traditional and online courses is that in an online course most of your communication will be written. You'll be emailing, using discussion boards and chat rooms, taking online tests, including essay exams, and interacting constantly throughout the semester with the instructor and other students. So, if your writing skills are poor, you're going to have difficulty in an online course. Here are some suggestions to help with online communication:

Discussion boards: respond to questions and posts in a timely manner. In almost all cases, there's a due date so that everyone has an opportunity to read posts, answer questions, and respond to the instructor and to other students in a timely manner. The best way to answer a post is to come up with some interesting facts and examples that will generate discussion. The best way to respond to another student's post is to comment in a way that will engage further dialogue and peak everyone's interest. Discussion boards are a great way to show your instructor that you're interested and involved.

Chat sessions: some online courses include chat sessions in which the instructor and the class participate in a discussion at the same time. This is a good way for the instructor to make sure that students are staying on top of the material and participating. If your course includes chat sessions, log in on time and contribute to the discussion.

Email: Online courses will require more emailing than usual, either between you and the instructor or with other students. When emailing, always include the course name in the subject line so that readers don't delete the email. When you receive an email from the instructor or another student, don't forward it on to someone else without their permission. Never use all capital letters, unless you want them to think you're yelling at them, and check your spelling and grammar so that your email is clear and understandable.

Personal conduct: internet etiquette is called "netiquette" and is important in all online communications. Instructors don't look very favorably on students who don't follow certain guidelines for internet conduct. Here are the main rules to follow:

Always be polite and respectful, and never criticize the instructor or other students.

Think before you write, since once you've sent something electronically you can't get it back.

Don't react negatively to someone else's email or discussion post.

Don't spam or send any unwanted messages or advertisements. Never forward someone else's email that they sent to you.

How to Take an Online Exam

Online exams can sometimes be more difficult than exams you take in a regular class because the instructor assumes that you will have access to books and other materials. Because of this, exams given online are usually more in-depth and require that you know the material really well. If you're not allowed to use any materials during the exam, then you're strictly on the honor system. Either way, there are precautions or rules you need to follow that will make taking online exams easier and much less stressful.

Before the exam

- **Have two browsers.** In some cases, one browser doesn't work as well for online sites such as Blackboard as another one does. Having two reliable browsers ensures that you'll be ready with a backup if problems arise.

- **Don't use a wireless connection.** Being wireless is great when you're just browsing the online site or reading discussions, but interference with nearby cell phones or other electronic devices can interrupt connections for an instant and disconnect you from the site. If you're in the middle of an exam, you'll be disconnected and lose valuable time. If at all possible, use a regular wired connection whenever you log into an exam.

- **Check your internet connection and speed.** First of all, if you have a dial up connection, you might run into problems with timed exams. So when taking your exams, find another computer with a cable or DSL connection. Also, before taking online exams, disable pop-up blockers since these can interfere with saving and submitting exams.

- **Reboot your computer before exams.** It's a good idea to close any programs that are running and then shut down your computer. When you turn it back on and log into the exam site, only single click anywhere you need to click. Double clicking may cause freezing up.

- **Read the instructions beforehand.** Your course syllabus or course information page should have your instructor's detailed exam policy. Read it carefully so that you know exactly how to take the exam, how much time you have, and whether you need to complete it once you begin or are allowed to stop and continue at a later time.

During the Exam

- **Read the questions carefully.** Once you click on the exam, questions will either come up one at a time or altogether. This is not the time to get flustered. Read each question carefully and use the test-taking techniques discussed in chapter 6.

- **Immediately contact your instructor with a problem.** Don't wait to report any technical problems that you encounter. First of all, if you wait too long you may not have as much time to finish the exam. And secondly, the instructor may have a rule that you need to report a problem within a certain period of time of experiencing it (thirty minutes, for example) so that the issue can be resolved in a timely manner.

- **Use a word processor for essay and short answer questions.** By using a standard word processing program like Microsoft Word, you're making a copy of your answer in case your computer goes down. Just copy and paste your answer into the online exam and then save the answer in Word. This may seem like a lot more work, but you'll be glad you did if your computer ever crashes and you need to redo your answers.

- **Review your answers.** In most cases, you'll be able to go back to any question and check your answers. Be careful not to navigate around or click on any other links. Remain on the test pages and you should be fine.

- **Save and submit.** Once you've completed the exam, click save and then submit one time. If you don't submit your exam, it won't be graded. Check your grade to make sure you successfully submitted your exam.

Some Final Don'ts

Taking online courses can be convenient, rewarding and fun. For some students it's the only way that they can go to school and complete their degree. Here are some final tips on how you can make the online experience as productive as possible.

1. Don't start the course blind and have to constantly ask the instructor for simple instructions that you should already have known about. Go over the entire online site before the class begins in order to get familiar with navigating all the pages.

2. Don't wait until the due date of an assignment or the day of an exam to get instructions. Ask for help immediately if there's anything you don't understand or can't find.

3. Don't assume that online exams are like exams you take in class. You'll be surprised, for example, when points are taken off for going over the time limit. So follow the posted rules and regulations for taking online exams.

4. Don't assume that just giving a one or two sentence answer on a discussion board if enough to impress your instructor. Remember, the discussion board is part of your grade and is also a way to make your teacher see you as an interested student.

5. Don't assume that your computer or internet will be reliable. By saving your assignments on a word processing program like Word, you'll always have a backup.

6. Don't assume that your instructor doesn't know how much time and effort you're putting into the course. It's very simple to go into the online course platform and check how often students log on, how much time they spend on exams, what time of day they log on, etc. So if you try and fool the instructor into thinking that you're doing what you're really not doing, it reflects on your work ethic and honesty.

Chapter 9

Time Management Skills

"To accomplish great things, we must not only plan but also believe."
- Anatole France, 1844-1924

Time management is the one of the most overlooked yet one of the most valuable skills you can learn early on during school because without knowing how to organize your life you'll never have the time to do what needs to be done to become a good student. Knowing how to manage your day-to-day activities will also carry over after you graduate, because unless you can manage time wisely, your career, no matter what it is, will be stressful, which will make your personal life stressful as well. By being efficient and well-organized from the start, you'll avoid the pitfalls most students fall into.

Learning how to manage your time can make the difference between you hating school and enjoying it because it will help you organize your life in a way that makes you a better and more productive student. And when you see that you're becoming more productive, you'll find yourself much happier, you'll handle daily stress much better, and you won't be as overwhelmed by the pressures that most students feel, especially during their first year.

How Good a Time Manager Are You?

Most of us have no idea whether we're good time managers or not. We assume we are because we've been conditioned to think that what we're doing is okay. The following time management quiz helps identify some of the problem areas you might have. Read each statement and then score it as follows: 1 = always; 2 = usually; 3 = sometimes; 4 = rarely. A scoring key at the end of the quiz will indicate how good a time manager you really are and which areas you need to work on.

I meet assignment deadlines	1	2	3	4
I keep a daily to-do list	1	2	3	4
I make time to get away from school	1	2	3	4
I write down specific goals and objectives	1	2	3	4
I set aside time each day for planning	1	2	3	4
I create schedules and try to keep them	1	2	3	4
I feel that I have control over my activities	1	2	3	4
I have a clear idea of what my day will be like	1	2	3	4
I am able to clear my work space by the end of the day	1	2	3	4
I set priorities for all my tasks	1	2	3	4
I include others in decision-making	1	2	3	4
I have no problem delegating responsibilities	1	2	3	4
I begin working on projects early	1	2	3	4
I am able to reschedule or eliminate low priority tasks	1	2	3	4
I feel that I am efficient and well-organized	1	2	3	4

I am clear about my duties and responsibilities	1	2	3	4
I know how much time I spend on various tasks	1	2	3	4
I leave time available in case the unexpected happens	1	2	3	4
I schedule more demanding tasks at peak energy levels	1	2	3	4
I finish one task before starting another	1	2	3	4
I find ways to cut down on duplicated effort	1	2	3	4
I keep up with new developments	1	2	3	4
I am able to identify sources of stress	1	2	3	4
I break large projects down into smaller projects	1	2	3	4
I am able to say no when pressed for time	1	2	3	4

Scoring key: 25-40: Excellent time manager

41-55: Good time manager

56-100: Poor time manager

If your quiz score tells you that you're a poor time manager, this chapter should be especially valuable in helping you organize your life. As a teacher, I've seen firsthand how frustrated, stressed, and burned out students get when they're poor time managers. They don't meet deadlines and they don't have enough hours in the day to study because they don't spend their time wisely and efficiently. As the school year rolls on, they keep falling behind, which only makes things worse. For most of these students, there are 10 common flaws that cause almost all of their problems. They are:

Not prioritizing tasks and assignments

Not being flexible enough to make room for more urgent tasks

Not scheduling daily, weekly, or monthly activities

Not writing down objectives in order to meet deadlines

Not using a calendar to organize commitments

Not reducing clutter and unnecessary paperwork

Not being able to avoid procrastination

Not taking a reasonable amount of credit hours

Not being able to say no

Not taking time for yourself

Because school life can often be challenging and overwhelming, it's important that you adopt time management techniques as soon as possible. I see it every day that I'm at school; students who do poorly on exams, who withdraw from classes, and even drop out of school simply because they never learned how to manage their time. Although not set in stone, the rule of thumb is that students should spend about 2 to 3 hours outside of class time reading, studying and doing various assignments and projects. That means 30 to 45 hours of work if you're taking 15 credits, which doesn't leave much room for much else unless you manage your time wisely.

In high school, with their parents help, students are pretty much told what they need to do and when to do it. In college, new found freedom can become a real issue. What I hear most from students are things like, "I don't have enough time," "I can't get myself organized," "I'm too distracted," "I'm under a lot of pressure," "I have so many other things I need to do." When I start to question some of my students about the use of their time, what I find in most cases is that they're overwhelmed by scheduling, planning, and organizing their activities and their school work. They simply have no idea how to manage their lives.

Time Management Strategies

Students have unique issues and problems to deal with that others don't. The following are proven strategies that have helped students in my classes for over 30 years. Some of these strategies may be common sense, but unless you make a conscientious effort to put them into practice every day, you won't become the expert student time manager you need to be.

- **Use a time planner.** Buy yourself a planner and include a list of your classes, exams, due dates, meetings, and social activities. Refer to it often to stay on track. Allow for unexpected interruptions, so leave a block of time available each day for unexpected meetings or sudden schedule changes. If an open block of time gets used, prioritize your other activities and reschedule tasks. By leaving yourself a little time each day, you'll become less anxious knowing that you'll always be able to schedule one more thing if you really need to.

- **Prioritize tasks.** One of the biggest time management thieves is not prioritizing. When deciding on what to do as you look through your planning book, ask yourself three questions before getting started:

Should I do it immediately?

Should I put if off until I have more time?

Should I eliminate it?

You can also assign your activities a priority ranking and do them according to your rakings:

Priority #1: Top priority. Activity needs to be done as soon as possible. Plan your schedule around the activity to meet deadlines.

Priority #2: High priority. Not as urgent but should be done soon. Activity is important enough to be put high on your schedule.

Priority #3: Low priority. Activity can wait until other higher priority activities are done.

Priority #4: Least priority. Not important or necessary. Activity should be placed last on your list or eliminated altogether.

- **Study wisely.** There are 7 specific time management rules for students to help them study much more effectively. They are:

Study in short sessions. Few of us can maintain full concentration for more than an hour. It's much more efficient to study in sessions of 45 minutes or so and then take a 15 minute break than it is to study for hours at a time.

Study during your peak energy levels. We all have unique biological clocks and energy levels at different times of the day. Identify if you're more of a morning, afternoon, or night person and schedule most of your study time then. If you can't decide when your best time is, alternate your study schedule and see what times of the day are the most effective.

Tackle the most difficult assignments when you're least tired. In order to maintain concentration and learn new material, make sure you're well rested and energized. You'll eliminate a lot of duplicated and wasted effort. Never study while in bed, and never study if you're distracted by something else.

Take time off. Taking time away from school work will reenergize you and reinvigorate your brain. Between sessions, relax and do something totally unrelated to school work.

Eliminate noise and other distractions. Despite what you may think, you will not be able to concentrate and learn as much as you can with the TV or radio playing. If your roommates are noisy, go to the library or find another quiet space. It may seem different at first to not have noise around you, but before you know it you'll find that quiet is much better for your mind.

Exercise and eat well. Staying physically fit does more than keep your body in shape; it keeps your mind sharp and helps you concentrate and focus. Good nutrition is also important in maintaining a healthy brain and a strong immune system.

Use flash cards. I always urge my students to use flash cards for every class I teach. Flash cards are an effective way to boil vital material down into short and manageable bits of information. Carry them around with you and refer to them between classes, while waiting for someone, during breaks, etc.

- **Schedule demanding tasks when you're most energized.** The most efficient students are those who recognize when their high energy levels are and adjust their schedules accordingly. It's always best to tackle the most demanding assignments first and leave easier tasks for the end of the day when you're tired and less energetic. Scheduling work in this way will make you feel good because you'll get the tough assignment out of the way and finish the day in a more pleasant mood.

- **Eliminate timewasters.** A time waster is any activity or behavior that is not necessary and that prevents you from accomplishing your goals. At the end of the day, it can sap your energy, create stress, and ruin your ability to manage time. Activities like going to every event, running errands, or talking to everyone who calls can take time away from more important tasks and leave you feeling frazzled. Make a commitment to eliminate the least important activities or, if necessary, put them at the end of your list and do them when you have nothing more important to do. The following is a list of the most common student timewasters:

Taking on additional or unnecessary duties

Having a cluttered or disorganized work space

Taking too many breaks

Reading unnecessary emails, texts, and/or spam

Spending too much time on the telephone

Spending too much time socializing

Surfing the web for non-school information

Not having adequate information to complete school work

Procrastinating

Sometimes you don't realize how much of what you do every day consists of unimportant or timewasting activities. Spending two hours on the phone with friends when you should be studying for exams, or playing video games between classes instead of going to the library to get started on a project leads to cramming at the last minute. Eliminating even a few of these activities increases your productivity to the point that you'll feel less stressed and more in control of your life.

- **Organize your work space.** To be a good time manager, eliminate clutter, put things in files, binders, and folders, and color code them for easy identification. The simple act of keeping your work space neat and clean and knowing where everything is will do wonders for your ability to get things done.

- **Write down and keep deadlines.** Over the years, I've given my share of bad grades to good students for not completing their assignments on time. A good teacher will make sure that his/her students know when assignments are due. The syllabus, which is a contract between teacher and student, should have all the deadlines you need to complete your work and get all the points available. So whenever you're given a deadline, write it down and then follow these rules:

Never put off a project that has a specific deadline. Procrastination makes deadlines impossible, so at least begin planning and outlining your work as soon as you get your assignment.

Allow yourself a few minutes from work every hour or so in order to catch your breath and clear your mind. It's always a good idea to take periodic breaks as long as you don't overdo it and get in the habit of wasting time by taking hour-long breaks every 30 minutes or so. When it's time to work, be disciplined. For instance, set up a schedule of one hour work and ten minutes of break and then stick to it.

Break projects down into smaller parts and set individual deadlines for each part. Taking things one step at a time helps you judge how well you are pacing yourself. More importantly, by looking at a project in stages, it won't seem so overwhelming. Writers, for example, concentrate on one chapter before going on to the next. Breaking a large assignment down into several parts will make your life a lot easier because you'll be following a specific plan of action that keeps you on track.

Don't put off making decisions. Effective decision-making helps you meet deadlines because you won't be waiting to get every single fact and piece of information possible before making a decision. There comes a time when you have to tell yourself that you have enough information to complete your assignment without having to waste more time looking for more material. There's a tendency that the longer you wait and the more information you try to gather, the harder it is to make a final decision. To avoid this "paralysis by analysis," follow these four steps:

1. **Write down the purpose or goal of the assignment**

2. **List the most important facts and information you'll need to complete the assignment**

3. **Get those facts and that information**

4. **Complete the assignment and meet the deadline using those facts and that information**

- **Finish one task before starting another.** Some of us can multitask fairly well; most of us can't. We might start something and then put it aside to finish later. In the meantime, we begin something new, and that's when things begin to pile up. Before we know it, we have a mound of work that needs to be done and we realize we don't have enough time to do it. Two of the biggest culprits are bad priority rankings and procrastination. To prevent this from ever happening, follow these two rules:

  Assign a priority ranking to every task. Look at your schedule and your daily planner and then shuffle around, reschedule, postpone, or eliminate the lowest priority tasks. Always begin high priority tasks immediately.

  Never procrastinate. Don't put off something because you might not like doing it or you think it may be time-consuming. If it needs to be done, start right away. Also, don't string lengthy assignments together. Intersperse long assignments with shorter ones to avoid boredom and fatigue.

- **Take control of your life.** Being in control of your day-to-day activities is as important in time management as it is in stress management. All the planning, scheduling, and organizing in the world isn't going to do any good unless you take charge over distractions and other activities that disrupt your day. In order to do that, here are some things to avoid:

  Avoid the telephone during study time. Chatting too much makes you lose touch of time and keeps you from staying on schedule. If you have to, tell your talkative friends that you're in the middle of something and that you'll call them back. Then check your schedule and use your down time to socialize.

Avoid unnecessary socializing. While some socializing is essential to keep you grounded and reduce stress, overdoing it wastes time and leads to bad habits. Before you know it, you'll be socializing more than studying, which always results in bad grades.

Avoid getting involved in others' activities. To be fully in control of your schedule, don't get involved with everything that others around you are doing. Sometimes you just have to remove yourself from activities, even if you really would like to get involved, if those activities take time away from more urgent and important tasks.

Avoid unorganized meetings and discussions. If you're meeting with other students about a class, make sure you have a plan. Know where it is, how long it will last, and what kinds of materials will be needed beforehand. If everyone is well prepared ahead of time, discussions will be controlled and to the point.

Avoid too many extracurricular activities. It's good to get involved in some activities, but don't overdo it. If you find that a certain activity begins to interfere with you study time or you're finding that you need to "fit in" study time, it's a sign that you need to pull back.

- **Don't take too many classes.** I see this as a real problem, especially with freshman. A full-time load is 12 credit hours, and a normal load that most students take in order to keep on track for their major is 15 credit hours. Some students will take 18 or more credits, thinking that they can handle that kind of load, and then run into all kinds of issues. Unless you're a genius, or some of those courses are really easy, don't overwhelm yourself with too many classes.

- **Write it down.** Being able to solve problems, accomplish goals, and finish assignments often depends on information you receive at the spur of the moment. Note-taking may not always be enough. There will be times when you'll need to jot down information when you don't have your notebook or you're away from class or your calendar. Always keep a pen or pencil and a small notepad with you wherever you go and get in the habit of using it when you have to. Once you're home, you can go through your notes and transcribe them into your notebook or calendar.

- **Improve reading and writing skills.** To be an effective time manager, you need to read quickly and with comprehension, and write well. Good readers know what to read, what to skim, and what to ignore altogether. By eliminating any unnecessary reading, you'll free up some of your time and be better able to plan your schedule with high priority activities. Good writers spend less time thinking about how to write and more time thinking about what to write. If you're writing skills are lacking, don't wait until your second or third year to take a writing course. Take one during your first semester so that you'll start off with a good foundation.

- **Learn to say no.** This is one of the best time management strategies you can use to avoid scheduling problems, eliminate timewasting activities, and stay in control of day-to-day planning and organizing. Saying yes to everything is stressful because it makes us feel as if everyone but us is making decisions. Delaying a decision is a good technique to use because it allows you to remove yourself from a situation and gives you time to find an excuse. When asked to do something, respond with "Let me check my schedule and get back with you." This gives you a chance to get out of committing right away and come up with a legitimate reason for saying no.

It's not what we do in the course of a school day that creates problems; it's how we do it. Whenever I ask students why they're so stressed out, at the top of the list are: not having enough time to do their work and feeling overwhelmed and overburdened. More than ever before, students feel that success comes at a high price; that there's so much competition for jobs that they need to work that much harder to have an advantage. One of the best ways to gain that advantage is to manage your time in a way that reduces the stress in your life and makes you a better student.

Chapter 10

Stress Management for Students

*"We must be willing to let go of the life we have planned
so as to have the life that is waiting for us."*

- E. M. Forster, 1879-1970

Today's students are experiencing more stress than at any time in history. New technologies, an increasing amount of information to learn, the pressure to get good grades, and global competition for jobs is making life more difficult and harder to cope with. It's hard enough for older adults to handle day-to-day stress; for students it can be one of the most trying and anxious times of their lives.

Given the amount of stress that many students are under while they're in school, it's not surprising that as many as 50 percent of all college students end up not graduating. In many cases, it's a lack of focus, poor time management or study skills, or just plain immaturity. Whenever I talk to students about the problems they're having, in almost all cases, they tell me how overwhelmed and stressed out they are. And that's why stress management for students is so important, especially early on and in particular when they feel the most at risk. Some common signs and symptoms of stress include:

Unusual headaches or recurring illnesses

Inability to control day-to-day activities

Increased anger and frustration

Change in sleeping patterns

Tense, tight muscles

Change in eating patterns

Inability to remember or concentrate

Hyperactivity and/or restlessness

Muscle twitching

Exhaustion

Experiencing some of the symptoms on the list may be a warning sign that you need to see a campus counselor. Be proactive. Don't wait until your stress is so bad that you feel as if you can't handle your school work any longer. Being a student is no different than being a worker in a stressful job. You need to admit that you're experiencing stress, recognize the source of that stress, and then do something about it before it gets out of hand.

Tips for Preventing School Stress

There are many ways to deal with stress, but for students it's important to use coping strategies that focus on school activities. One of the worst things about school stress is that it can build up over time and begin to overwhelm even the best students. The following tips will help keep you from getting stressed in the first place.

- **Visit your academic advisor early and often.** Many new students get frustrated and stressed out because they don't have goals or a long-range plan. They're not sure about what classes to take, they don't have direction, and they don't understand the prerequisites and core requirements for their major. I run into this every semester. So make sure that you know who your advisor is and then make regular visits to his/her office with any questions and concerns you have. Make it a habit of seeing your advisor every semester.

- **Ease up on your extracurricular activities.** While extracurricular activities look good on a resume, and can increase your social support network, too many will interfere with scheduling and study time. Choose your extracurricular activities wisely. Select the ones that you enjoy but also ones that are associated with your major and will enhance your resume and future job prospects. For example, if you're a premed student and you have to choose between 3 nights of intramural bowling or the medical student association, it's a no brainer that you should choose the latter.

- **Don't keep things bottled up.** Expressing your feelings and emotions has a dramatic effect on how well you cope with life events. By talking things out and not allowing stress to fester, you'll handle any situation much better. When talking things out, find the positive among the negatives. If you only dwell on the negative, your stress will only get worse.

- **Make time for physical activity.** Spend 30 minutes three times a week doing some kind of physical activity. Exercise is important because it rejuvenates the body and stimulates the mind. Your brain depends on the body to release hormones and chemicals that build resistance, fight disease, and enhance performance. When you become inactive, your energy levels drop and you naturally become more prone to stress.

- **Take time to relax.** Find a quiet place you can go to each day and just relax. Everyone, no matter how much they love what they're doing or how stress tolerant they think they are, needs time to recover from work and study. Walking, running, or just getting up and going to the gym will stimulate both your nervous and immune systems and give you a sense of well-being and will have a positive effect on your attitude.

- **Learn relaxation techniques.** One of the most important pieces of advice I give to anyone who wants to eliminate the stress in their lives is to set aside time for relaxation exercises. At the end of the chapter, I'll outline some of the best ways to use relaxation exercises to cope with stress and bring your body back into what I call "relaxed equilibrium."

- **Ease up on your course load.** This has got to be the single biggest source of student stress. Not only is it stressful to take four or five difficult classes, it makes scheduling and managing your time a nightmare. There's no reason for you to take 18 or more credit hours, especially if you're going to end up doing poorly in some classes and may even have to take them over. Believe me, once you graduate, it's your grades that will land you an interview and a job, not the fact that you crammed in a lot of classes every semester. Personally, I would rather hire someone who took 12 credits a semester and graduated in 5 years with a 3.75GPA than someone who took 18 credit hours a semester and ended up with a 2.5 GPA. If you fall behind, you can always make up some work by taking summer classes.

- **Eat the right foods.** There was a popular saying some years ago, "*You are what you eat.*" What you eat has a direct effect on how you feel, how well you cope with stress, and how well you maintain your immune system, which can break down if you're stressed out. Foods high in saturated fats can make you sluggish and clog your arteries; and refined sugar, found in foods like white bread, white rice, soda, and most snacks, spike your insulin levels. More insulin means more fat deposits, as well as a bigger appetite, which leads to overeating. Some foods, labeled "high stress foods" can make stress worse; others can help you fight stress and keep you healthy during those times when you need it most.

Foods that fight stress

Beans, brown rice, chicken breast (not fried), cottage cheese, low fat milk, fish, fruit (especially apples, bananas, cantaloupe, oranges, and pineapple), legumes, nuts, oatmeal, soybeans, sunflower seeds, turkey breast, vegetables (especially dark green leafy vegetables), wheat germ, whole grain cereal, whole wheat bread

High stress foods to avoid

Cake, candy, cold cuts (except for low fat meats like turkey and chicken breast without nitrates), doughnuts, soda, fried foods, meats high in saturated fat, sweet rolls, white pasta, white rice, whole milk, white bread

Coping with Burnout

Although it can have similar symptoms, burnout isn't really the same as stress; it's the result of exposure to stress over a long period of time. Students who have trouble coping with school and who are stressed out day in and day out will eventually get burned out and may even drop out of school. One of the side effects of burnout is that it often causes physical illness, which then leads to even more stress.

Although burnout can happen to anyone, students who are most vulnerable are the ones who are under constant pressure and who find that they just can't find the time to do everything that's required. Typical character traits are perfectionists, idealists, workaholics, and those who can't say no.

How do you know if you're beginning to experience burnout? The following burnout rating quiz is a good way to determine your burnout index. Read each response and rate is as: 1 = always; 2 = sometimes; 3 = seldom or never. A scoring key at the end of the quiz will tell you how prone you are to burnout.

I feel that each day is a good day	1	2	3
I have enough time for myself during the day	1	2	3
I have good balance in my life	1	2	3
I feel energized when studying and doing assignments	1	2	3
I feel successful about what I do	1	2	3
I get along with my fellow students	1	2	3
I feel well-rested and refreshed	1	2	3
I get at least 7 hours of sleep a night	1	2	3
I have a sense of accomplishment about what I do	1	2	3
I am organized and efficient	1	2	3
I feel productive	1	2	3
I take time off periodically from school work	1	2	3

I feel that I'm able to speak up and criticize	1	2	3
I feel excited about going to classes	1	2	3
I feel like my teachers care about what I do	1	2	3
I have no problem adapting to change	1	2	3
I'm in a good mood when I get home	1	2	3
I feel that school gives me satisfaction	1	2	3
I have a positive outlook on life	1	2	3
I participate in school-related events	1	2	3
I consider myself a dedicated student	1	2	3
I feel like what I do makes a difference	1	2	3
I am able to plan and schedule my work	1	2	3
I get together with friends or family	1	2	3
I am motivated and enthusiastic	1	2	3

Scoring key: 25-39: You are healthy and not experiencing burnout

40-59: You have early signs of moderate burnout

60-75: You have severe burnout and need counseling

Burnout has a profound effect on study habits and learning, so recognizing and eliminating the causes of burnout as soon as possible is important if you want to make school life as stress-free and enjoyable as possible. Here are some specific ways to prevent burnout from happening in the first place.

- **Don't be a perfectionist.** Since perfection doesn't exist, trying to be perfect can lead to stress, depression, and eventually burnout. It's okay to try and be the best you can be; but you need to come to grips with the fact that there will always be things you can't do as well as you'd like.

- **Take advantage of your biological clock.** Recognize your own personal energy levels and schedule the most demanding or stressful tasks during those times. If you try to work on something stressful when you have the least energy, you'll get tired much faster and get frustrated because you won't be as efficient in doing the work. Spend an entire week working on assignments during various times of the day and evening and you'll quickly discover when your peak energy levels are. Once you do, stick to your biological clock and watch your stress levels go down.

- **View change as rewarding and challenging.** In most cases, change is not something we view positively because many of us are not really very good at it. Mostly it's a fear of the unknown or the fear of failure. So rather than seeing change as something bad that happens to you, look for the positives and see it as an opportunity to experience something new and different.

- **Take control over situations.** Having a feeling of control over your life is one of the most important attitudes you can have if you want to prevent stress and burnout. Studies have shown that we get sick, not because of stressful situations, long hours, and deadlines but because we feel that what we're doing or nor doing is beyond our control. To reverse that, get involved rather than sit passively by and have others take charge. So join, participate, volunteer, and become active. Doing whatever you can to lead instead of follow will make you feel more in control.

- **Learn to say no.** I'm sure you've been told that your resume needs to have more on it than just your school work. You need extracurricular activities. But taking on extra work that isn't required will eventually cause feelings of anger, resentment, and frustration. Not being able to say no makes you feel helpless and out of control. Instead of saying yes to everything, be selective and choose the things you really want to be involved in and which will improve your grades.

- **Cut projects down to size.** The mind likes to compartmentalize. Most of us don't, and so we get overwhelmed by large projects. An effective way to compartmentalize is to reduce a project down to its individual parts so that it's easier to handle. When writing this book, for example,

I broke it down first into chapters and then into sections within each chapter and went on from there. By working on one smaller section at a time, a project won't seem difficult at all.

- **Always try to exceed your expectations.** Every semester I tell my students to never be satisfied doing only what's expected of them, and to always strive to exceed expectations. If a student does 5 percent more than what's expected, he/she will be better than 90 percent of the population. So if you want to prevent burnout and succeed in the process, go out of your way to improve yourself, take on challenges, and strive to be the best you can be at whatever you do.

The common misconception about burnout is that it develops quickly and without warning. In reality, it could take years before burnout affects someone physically and emotionally. In fact, just last semester, I talked to a senior who seemed fine during her first few years of school but who was now experiencing severe stress and burnout. The good news is that students who seek counseling early and get the help they need, can easily prevent stress in the first place. By learning time management and relaxation techniques, and following the guidelines for coping with school, they will never experience burnout.

School Stress and Depression

Depression is a medical condition that may involve mood swings, sadness, insomnia, weight loss, guilt, and a lack of response to one's surroundings. We all experience these signs and symptoms at one time or another because we all react to stress differently. Your depression can be as simple as sadness over a loss or as severe as deep withdrawal where you isolate yourself from others and find it impossible to function normally. The difference is that one is temporary while the other usually involves a chemical imbalance that needs to be treated by a physician.

Depression that goes on for a few weeks or months is called "clinical depression," which is far more than the ordinary down moods that everyone experiences now and then and that often pass after a visit with a friend. Clinical depression is a medical disorder that affects how we think and feel, and it should always be taken seriously, since it can lead to even deeper depression and thoughts of suicide. If you experience three or more of the following symptoms for more than a few days, go to the counseling center and ask for help.

Persistent sadness and/or feelings of emptiness

Decreased energy level; becoming fatigued more often

Loss of interest or pleasure in day-to-day activities

Sleep problems (insomnia, oversleeping, early morning waking)

Difficulty concentrating, remembering, or making decisions

Feelings of hopelessness or pessimism

Feelings of guilt, worthlessness, or helplessness

Loss of appetite or weight; weight gain

Thoughts of death or suicide or attempts at suicide

Increased anger, moodiness, or irritability

Excessive crying, sometimes for no apparent reason

A simple way to know if you're just having a few bad days or are truly suffering with depression is to take the following depression rating quiz. The answer key at the end will give you an idea of whether or not you're truly suffering with depression.

1. Have you lost interest in things you once enjoyed? Yes ☐ No ☐

2. Do you feel sad or blue every day? Yes ☐ No ☐

3. Are you lethargic or unable to sit still? Yes ☐ No ☐

4. Do you have feelings of guilt or worthlessness? Yes ☐ No ☐

5. Has your appetite increased or decreased suddenly? Yes ☐ No ☐

6. Do you have thoughts of death or suicide? Yes ☐ No ☐

7. Do you have trouble concentrating? Yes ☐ No ☐

8. Do you have insomnia or do you sleep too much? Yes ☐ No ☐

9. Are you tired all of the time? Yes ☐ No ☐

10. Do you worry about things much of the time? Yes ☐ No ☐

11. Do you feel pessimistic or hopeless? Yes ☐ No ☐

12. Have you started drinking more often? Yes ☐ No ☐

13. Do you have unexplained pains and/or aches? Yes ☐ No ☐

14. Do you have digestive problems more often? Yes ☐ No ☐

15. Are you angry or moody more than usual? Yes ☐ No ☐

Scoring key:

If you answered YES to either question 1 or 2 and your symptoms have lingered for more than just a few days, you are suffering with depression. If the symptoms have persisted for at least a week, you need to seek counseling as soon as possible.

If you answered YES to "at least" three of the next seven questions (questions 3-9), chances are you might be suffering from depression, especially if the symptoms have lasted several days. You may want to consider seeing a counselor to discuss your issues.

If you answered YES to the remaining 5 questions (questions 10-15), there's a good chance you are suffering from depression.

Treating Stress-Related Depression

In male students, depression is often masked by alcohol, drug abuse, or working excessively long hours. Men are more likely to have feelings of hopelessness, anger, frustration, resentment, and discouragement and less likely to admit that they are depressed. Women, on the other hand, experience depression twice as often as men but are more willing to admit that they are depressed, and they seek help more often. Hormones can contribute to increased depression in women, especially during their menstrual cycles.

Unless your depression is severe and lasts longer than a few days or more than a week, it's probably the result of stress, anxiety, and overwork. It's not unusual for students to get so stressed out that they begin to feel tired all the time, helpless, and out of control. The following are some effective coping techniques to get you out of your funk and back into a normal routine:

- **Get in the habit of thinking positively.** Having a negative attitude is a habit you acquire over a lifetime. Sometimes it develops as a result of being around negative family members or friends. The more you focus on the negative, the more you condition yourself to develop a negative personality that makes you more prone to depression. You can train yourself to think positively and become happier by simply refocusing on the positive aspects of your life and being grateful for what you have. Remind yourself how lucky you are for the things that make your life special. Take a moment each day to sit back and think about what's good about your life.

- **Visualize positive results.** One of the most common behaviors that cause stress, anxiety, and illness is something called "spectatoring." As if you're looking through someone else's eyes, you visualize what's happening to you or what will happen to you, and you don't like what you see. Performance anxiety is common when you're about to give a speech or perform before a group. In fact, speaking in public is the number one fear that people have. To rid yourself of this negative habit, close your eyes and imagine success instead of failure. Doing this often enough will condition your brain to start visualizing positive outcomes.

- **Learn time management skills.** In the previous chapter, I emphasized how important time management is for helping you schedule your life, study more effectively, and get better grades. But time management is also critical for reducing stress and burnout because it de-clutters your life and makes everything you do much more manageable. Unless you can manage your time wisely, you're always going to feel tired, stressed out, and overwhelmed.

- **Don't dwell on the past.** Don't get caught up in past events. Dwelling too much on previous mistakes or failures, on what you should have done, or what you should have said or not said, conditions the brain to intensify those negative thoughts the next time. The past is over, and the only thing you can do is learn from it, work on the present, and prepare for the future. Instead of worrying about what should have been, use your past experience as a tool for focusing on your next accomplishment. The greatest achievers and the most successful people in life all have one thing in common: they all learn from past mistakes and they all use failure as an incentive to accomplish what they set out to do.

- **Stress-proof your surroundings.** Your environment and the things that surround you have a profound effect on how you feel and how energized you are. If you enjoy listening to music, listen only to the type of music that makes you feel most relaxed, not the music that's currently popular or that you think you should be listening to because everyone else is. Surround yourself with photos or paintings you enjoy looking at, and with color schemes that are soothing rather than stimulating. Natural light and plants also improve study and learning.

- **Expand your circle of friends.** Seeing friends and family regularly can do wonders for your mental health. Without sacrificing study time and deadlines, schedule get-togethers, have game nights, watch a ball game, and enjoy your time off. Students can become lonely and depressed, especially if they're away from home for the first time; and one of the best ways to overcome depression and loneliness is to reach out to others instead of expecting others to reach out to you. The healthiest students are the ones who have a network of friends and see them on a regular basis.

- **Become more involved.** Becoming involved in activities is a great way to meet interesting people and start to build social support networks. It's also a good way to develop interpersonal skills that you'll need after you graduate, and will be a good addition to your resume. Volunteering at a hospital, homeless shelter, senior services, or a civic organization, for example, is not only a noble thing to do, it gives you a sense of worth and accomplishment and makes you realize how truly fortunate you are. Be careful, though, about how involved you get. Too much extracurricular activities and you're likely to start neglecting your school work.

- **Exercise regularly.** There's more to exercise than simply getting fit. Regular exercise energizes us, boosts the immune system, helps us sleep better, gives us a feeling of health and well-being, and helps us relax. Stimulating the body refreshes the mind. Your brain needs activity by the rest of your body in order to revitalize the senses and keep you in a good state of balance. An added benefit, based on a study done at Duke University, is that if you exercise at least 3 times a week, you're just as likely to recover from depression as those who are using antidepressants.

Relaxation Techniques

One of the cornerstones of any effective stress management strategy is relaxation. There are many relaxation techniques that work really well, but each individual needs to find out which technique they prefer and which one works best for them. Try them all for a week and then practice the one you like best. The more you use a specific technique, the better you'll get at it, and the more effective it will be.

Meditation

For centuries, meditation has been the choice for achieving peace of mind by conditioning the brain to trigger the relaxation response. The benefits of meditation start almost immediately. Once you begin meditating, your heart rate and blood pressure decrease and your energy levels increase. Students who meditate every day say that they feel more refreshed and invigorated. In order to achieve a state of deep relaxation, you need to follow some rules:

1. **Find a quiet location.** It's impossible to relax and focus with all sorts of distractions around you. For meditation to work, you need quiet and comfort because the basic component of meditation is attention and concentration. So choose a quiet room, a peaceful garden, or any place where you know that you won't be interrupted for at least fifteen minutes.

2. **Make sure you're comfortable.** Wear loose clothing, loosen your belt, take off your shoes, undo some buttons, and don't eat a large meal beforehand. Sit in a comfortable chair with your head, neck, and back held upright but not rigid. Place your feet flat on the floor and your hands held loosely and facing palm up on your lap.

3. **Choose a specific time and place to meditate.** Morning is great because it starts your day. Evening is also good because it helps you wind down. In any case, meditate regularly, even if you don't feel like it. Ten minutes is better than none.

4. **Free your mind of distractions.** Since meditation is a relaxation technique, free your mind and allow it to remain quiet with no intrusive thoughts. As you meditate, remain calm and passive and allow distracting thoughts to simply melt away. The most effective way to do that is use a mental device or "mantra."

5. **Use a focus of attention.** A mantra is a sound, a word or a phrase repeated aloud or silently and used to focus attention and keep distracting thoughts from interfering with meditation. Other ways to focus may include an object like a candle flame, a breath, or even a body part.

6. **Breathe properly.** Close your mouth, place your tongue along the roof of your mouth, and breathe slowly through your nose. Don't force breathing; just become aware of your breaths as they enter and leave your body. Also, don't take short or rapid breaths because this leads to tension.

Meditation using a word

Sit quietly in any comfortable position, close your eyes, and breathe through your nose. Inhale slowly and smoothly for five seconds. As you exhale, say the word *"relax"* or *"one"* to yourself. Let the word flow with your breath, feeling the tension melting away and your muscle becoming more relaxed with each exhalation. Continue this for five to ten minutes at first and work your way up to fifteen to twenty minutes. When you finish, sit quietly for a few minutes before getting up and stretching a bit before going on to your normal routine.

Meditation using a sound

This meditation exercise uses a sound that synchronizes your breathing with the sound. I like to use a metronome that you can adjust to a setting that mirrors your breathing pattern. Once your breathing begins to follow the beat of the metronome, begin to concentrate on the sound of the clicks, saying the word *"relax"* at the same pace as both your breathing and the clicking. After several weeks of using this technique, your brain will become conditioned and automatically associate the clicks with relaxation and your body with instantly trigger the relaxation response.

Meditation using autosuggestion

This exercise is like self-hypnosis, and it's similar to the previous technique in that your brain is conditioned to trigger relaxation at the sound of a number. In this exercise, find a quiet location, sit in a comfortable position, and begin to breathe smoothly and rhythmically. Then, starting with the number ten, begin counting backwards, one number for each exhalation. As you count, feel your body getting more and more relaxed.

By the time you reach the number five, feel your eyelids becoming heavy, starting to blink, and finally closing. When you get to number one, feel your entire body become heavy and go limp with relaxation, and then remain that way for ten minutes. At the end of the session, count slowly from one to three, taking a smooth, deep breathe at each count. When you get to three, slowly open your eyes, stand up, and stretch for a few seconds. Once you've done this for several weeks, your body will automatically associate the number five with eye closing and the number one with your body going limp.

Visualization

This type of relaxation technique, also known as imaging or guided imagery, uses mental images to achieve a deeply relaxed state. It's one of the most popular techniques used because it's simple to learn, enjoyable, and very effective. With visualization, you use specific and vivid mental images as a way to stimulate your nervous system to relax your muscles. Once practiced, the images you visualize will trigger a physical response that puts you into a relaxed state. As with meditation, you need to follow some general guidelines to make this technique more effective.

1. **Get comfortable.** First and foremost, visualization is a relaxation technique; so just as you would with meditation, make comfort a priority. Distractions like muscle tension, tight clothing or jewelry, and improper room temperature will interfere with concentration and your ability to maintain an image for any length of time. If you're sitting, don't cross your arms or legs; if you're lying down, make sure you use a comfortable pillow.

2. **Breathe properly.** Smooth, even, and rhythmic breathing is essential to effective guided imagery. Make sure that your breathing is natural and not forced. As you breathe, your stomach should be moving in and out, not your chest.

3. **Use familiar images.** The most powerful images are ones that are familiar to you; ones from your own personal experiences and places you've visited. It's much harder to maintain an image that you have to make up than one that pops into your head because you're already familiar with it. The brain is good at storing information from your past, so take advantage of that. Real is always better than contrived.

4. **Make images vivid and animated.** Memory experts use tricks to help people remember facts. One of those tricks is to make mental images animated. For example, if your mental image is one of you lying on a beach, make the water gently lap along the shore and the warm breeze blow across your body. Dull, static images are never as powerful or memorable as ones that are vividly colorful and dynamic.

5. **Choose images wisely.** It's a mistake thinking that a familiar image is going to work for you. What if you hate the beach, for instance? Or hate the idea of the sun beating down on you? Nothing is going to be more distracting and ineffective than using an image that will actually cause you tension and anxiety. Experiment, and soon you'll find the perfect image that evokes pleasure and relaxation almost immediately.

Visualization Exercise

Close your eyes and breathe slowly and smoothly. With each breathe, feel your muscles becoming heavier and heavier . . . more relaxed with each breath. Feel the tension melting away as you breathe smoothly, rhythmically, and naturally. Once you're sufficiently relaxed, begin these self-guided images:

Imagine yourself lying on a warm, tropical beach, basking in the glow of an afternoon sun. The sun's rays are radiating over every inch of your body, while the warmth of the sand is penetrating your pores. The vivid, beautiful colors of the sky, earth, flowers, and plants are all around you. Now feel the warmth of the golden sand getting more intense, penetrating even deeper into every pore of your body as it makes you feel warmer and warmer . . . more relaxed as you breathe deeply and smoothly. The golden sand feels soft and soothing . . . its warmth enters into your fingers and toes and then into your hands and feet as it begins to creep throughout your entire body.

Feel your muscles becoming loose and limp . . . and sense all the tension melting away. You feel your body becoming heavier and heavier, sinking into the sand and drifting deeper and deeper into a state of peace and total relaxation. With each breath you take, your body is becoming more and more relaxed . . . more and more at peace. As you breathe, feel your chest getting warmer and more relaxed.

Feel the warmth of the sunlight all over your body, warming you deeply and gently. Imagine the inside of your body bathed in the golden light, absorbing every ray and glowing as radiantly as the sun. A warm, gentle breeze is swirling around your body and warms you even more. Feel the warm breeze blowing over every part of your body and making you relax . . . relax . . . relax.

Progressive Muscle Relaxation

Progressive muscle relaxation or PMR gradually relaxes your muscles, one body part at a time, until you achieve a deeply relaxed state. Your muscles are trained, through autosuggestion and brain conditioning, to relax spontaneously in response to a set of instructions. When doing PMR, loosen your clothing, sit in a comfortable chair or lie down and begin to breathe slowly and smoothly. Use soft words like relax, soothing, smooth, numb, and limp. Avoid harsh sounding words that are distracting and cause you to lose your focus. Don't rush the exercise. Moving from one body part to the next too quickly disrupts the flow of PMR and makes the exercise less effective.

PMR Exercise

Close your eyes and, beginning with your feet, concentrate on one muscle group at a time. After a few weeks of brain conditioning, relaxation will come more quickly and with much less effort because you'll be developing a habit that becomes ingrained in your subconscious. Certain words like relax numb and heavy will automatically begin to trigger the relaxation response. The goal of PMR is to induce a state of complete relaxation within a few minutes of starting an exercise. Here is an example of a PMR exercise:

"I'm falling into a relaxed state as I breathe deeply, slowly, and smoothly . . . deeply, slowly, and smoothly. As I breathe, I'm becoming more and more relaxed . . . relaxed . . . relaxed. The toes on my feet are becoming numb. I feel a tingling sensation as the muscles in my toes become more relaxed . . . relaxed . . . relaxed. My toes feel numb and heavy . . . numb and heavy . . . relaxed . . . relaxed . . . relaxed . . . more relaxed with each breath I take."

"The numbness is creeping into my feet. My feet are beginning to tingle and are heavy and numb . . . heavy and numb. There's a burning sensation in my feet as if they're in warm water. As I breathe, I feel my feet becoming numb and more relaxed . . . relaxed . . . relaxed . . . loose and soft . . . loose and soft. They feel warm, heavy, and relaxed . . . relaxed . . . relaxed . . . more relaxed with each breathe I take. My feet are so warm and soft . . . warm and soft and relaxed . . . relaxed . . . relaxed . . . more relaxed with each breathe I take."

"I feel the warmth and numbness going up into my calves as I breathe and relax . . . breathe and relax . . . relax . . . relax . . . relax. My calves are getting heavy and numb . . . heavy and numb and relaxed. They're getting soft and warm as tension leaves and muscles relax . . . relax . . . relax. With each breath I take, my calves are getting heavier . . . heavier . . . heavier . . . relaxed and numb . . . relaxed . . . relaxed . . . relaxed . . . more relaxed with each breathe I take."

"The numbness is moving into my thighs. My thighs feel warm and soft . . . warm and soft . . . loose and relaxed . . . relaxed . . . relaxed. There's a tingling sensation as they become numb and heavy . . . numb and heavy and relaxed . . . relaxed . . . relaxed. With each breathe I take, my thighs are getting more and more relaxed and heavier . . . heavier . . . heavier. I feel the warmth and numbness creeping up my thighs and releasing tension. With each breathe I take, my thighs feel heavy and limp . . . limp and relaxed . . . relaxed . . . relaxed . . . more relaxed with each breathe I take."

"My fingers are tingling and getting numb as the warmth creeps into them. They're now soft and loose . . . soft and loose . . . warm and numb . . . numb . . . numb. I sense the numbness going from my fingers into my knuckles as I breathe slowly and relax . . . relax . . . relax. The warmth and numbness is going into my wrists and my wrists are getting warmer and warmer . . . softer and softer. My hands are heavy and relaxed . . . relaxed . . . relaxed. With each breath I take, my hands are heavy and relaxed . . . relaxed . . . relaxed . . . more relaxed with each breath I take."

"My arms are beginning to bet numb. The warmth is spreading from my hands into my arms and I feel heaviness and warmth . . . heaviness and warmth. As I breathe, my arms are getting heavier and heavier . . . numb and relaxed . . . relaxed . . . relaxed. A tingling is going up my arms and releasing tension. My arms are heavy and relaxed . . . relaxed . . . relaxed . . . more relaxed with each breathe I take."

"The numbness is creeping into my shoulders and my shoulders are getting numb and heavy . . . numb and heavy . . . numb and heavy. I feel the warmth and heaviness loosening the muscles in my shoulders as they become more relaxed . . . relaxed . . . relaxed . . . more relaxed with each breath I take. As I breathe, tension is flowing out of my shoulders as they feel so warm and numb . . . warm and numb . . . heavy and relaxed . . . relaxed . . . relaxed . . . relaxed . . . more relaxed with each breath I take."

"Warmth is spreading into my chest as I breathe deeply and it feels warmer and warmer . . . looser and looser. With each breath I take, my chest is more loose, heavy, and numb . . . soft and relaxed . . . relaxed . . . relaxed . . . relaxed. I feel the muscles in my chest tingling and becoming numb and heavy. As I breathe, tension is leaving my chest, which is heavy and relaxed . . . relaxed . . . relaxed . . . more relaxed with each breathe I take."

"The numbness is moving from my chest into my neck. My neck is becoming loose and soft . . . warm and numb . . . warm and numb. I feel the tingling, numbing feeling in my neck as I breathe and relax . . . relax . . . relax. My neck is heavier and heavier . . . warmer and warmer . . . more relaxed with each breath I take. The tension is melting away from my neck and I feel so relaxed . . . relaxed . . . relaxed . . . more relaxed with each breath I take."

"My body feels so warm and relaxed . . . relaxed . . . heavy and numb . . . heavy and numb. My body is so heavy and relaxed. Tension is melting away; my muscles are soft and relaxed . . . soft and relaxed . . . heavy and limp . . . heavy and limp. As I breathe, I feel soothing warmth washing over my body and I'm totally relaxed . . . relaxed . . . relaxed . . . relaxed . . . relaxed."

One of the great things about PMR is that once you've conditioned your body to listen to your brain, relaxation becomes almost spontaneous. As with any physiological reaction, the mind-body connection is geared toward responding to your brain's instructions. Once you learn how your muscles should feel when they're relaxed, it becomes a simple matter of habit and conditioning to bring them into that relaxed state whenever you want to.

Alternative Relaxation Techniques

For most students, meditation, visualization, and/or Progressive Muscle Relaxation are all successful strategies for reducing stress. For other students, less common techniques like the ones described in this section work more effectively. The decision to use alternative techniques is usually a last resort, but can be a great way to help in dealing with stress and anxiety. The following are some of the most popular and successful alternative techniques.

Aromatherapy

Aromatherapy is the use of essential oils for relaxation and stress relief or to treat headaches, pain, circulatory problems, and indigestion. It can also affect mood and behavior. In theory, aromatherapy works by stimulating the brain to release certain beneficial hormones while inhibiting damaging ones like cortisol. The most common oils are used as muscle relaxants, and the five best ones are: lavender, peppermint, eucalyptus, chamomile, jasmine, and rosemary.

Color and Light Therapy

When cells in the retina of the eye are stimulated by certain colors and light, they send nerve impulses to the brain that decrease tension, enhance learning and memory, fight depression and fatigue, and actually speed up the healing process. Greens and blues, for example, calm and soothe (that's why hospital walls are often painted these colors). Reds and oranges stimulate, which is why many fast food restaurants use these colors. So to help you relax, think about surrounding yourself with warm and soothing colors.

Music Therapy

Since ancient times, music and musical instruments have been used to soothe, relax, and influence health and well-being. The first official music therapy degree program was founded at Michigan State University in 1944; and since then graduates have been working at hospitals, clinics, health centers, and other health facilities. You don't need the help of an expert to use music therapy for relaxation. All you need is a CD player and a few discs with soft, soothing music. When you feel overwhelmed and stressed, pop in a CD, sit back in a comfortable chair or lie in a warm bath, close your eyes, and allow your mind and your body to relax.

Yoga

The goal of Yoga is to attain higher consciousness and spiritual realization. But besides the spiritual aspect of the discipline, Yoga reduces stress and improves physical fitness through stretching and muscle strengthening, meditation, and breathing. If you want to learn Yoga and benefit from its many positive effects, sign up for a class or buy a CD and try it in the comfort of your home.

Therapeutic Humor

Ever since Norman Cousins, author of the bestseller *Anatomy of an Illness*, cured himself of a serious, debilitating disease by watching hours of comedy shows, laughter has been used as a way to relax and heal. In fact, humor and laughter have been associated with health since biblical times. Proverbs 17:22 states that "A merry heart doeth good like medicine." The ancient Greeks built hospitals next to amphitheaters because they knew that patients would heal faster if they watched comedies. So don't take everything so seriously. Go out with friends, see a funny movie, and have a good laugh. All the evidence we have points to the fact that a good belly laugh is also great medicine.

Chapter 11

Keeping Your Mind & Body Healthy

"The future belongs to those who believe in the beauty of their dreams."
- Eleanor Roosevelt, 1884-1962

There's a worry among some health professionals that school, especially the first year of school, may be bad for your health. That's because students are usually too busy to eat the right foods, get enough exercise, and take care of their mental and physical health in general. Unfortunately, this can translate into poor study habits and then poor grades. As the semester progresses, they get more and more stressed out and they put their health needs at the bottom of their list of priorities. Before long, this neglect becomes a habit that leads to more serious health problems. This chapter will help you change that.

Health Assessment Quiz

How healthy do you think you are? What things do you do that make school life hazardous to your health? What behaviors can you change to become a better student? I'm sure that few students ask themselves these sorts of questions. Despite having access to more health information than ever, many of us don't know what to do to be as healthy as possible.

Lifestyle is one of the most important factors affecting health, and students often choose poor lifestyles and neglect their health at a time when they're most at risk.

The following test, designed by the Public Health Service, will tell you how well you're doing. Read each question and then circle the number that corresponds to the following answer: 0 = almost never; 1 = sometimes, 2, 3, or 4 = almost always.

Cigarette Smoking			
If you never smoke, enter a score of **10** for this section and go on to the next section on alcohol and drugs			
I avoid smoking cigarettes	2	1	0
I smoke cigarettes, a pipe, or a cigar	2	1	0
Smoking score: _____			
Alcohol and Drugs			
I avoid drinking alcoholic beverages or I drink no more than one or two drinks a day	4	1	0
I avoid alcohol or other drugs, especially illegal drugs, as a way of handling stress or the problems in my life	2	1	0
I am careful not to drink alcohol when taking certain medicines (examples: medicines for sleeping, pain, colds, and allergies) or when pregnant.	2	1	0
I read and follow the label directions when using prescribed and over-the-counter drugs.	2	1	0
Alcohol and drugs score: _____			

Eating Habits			
I eat a variety of foods each day, such as vegetables and fruits, whole grain breads and cereals, lean meats, dairy products, beans, and nuts and seeds.	4	1	0
I limit the amount of fat, saturated fat, and cholesterol I eat, including fat on meats, butter, cream, shortenings, and organ meats such as liver.	2	1	0
I limit the amount of salt I eat by cooking with only small amounts, not adding salt at the table, and avoiding salty snacks.	2	1	0
I avoid eating too much sugar, especially frequent snacks of candy or soft drinks.	2	1	0
Eating habits score: _____			
Exercise & Fitness			
I maintain a desired weight, avoiding being overweight and underweight.	3	1	0
I do vigorous exercises for 5 to 30 minutes at least 3 times a week (example: running, swimming, brisk walking).	3	1	0
I do exercises that enhance my muscle tone for 15 to 30 minutes at least 3 times a week (examples: yoga and calisthenics).	2	1	0
I use part of my leisure time participating in individual or team activities that increase my level of fitness, such as bowling, golf, and softball.	2	1	0
Exercise & fitness score: _____			

Stress Control			
I have a job or do other work that I enjoy.	2	1	0
I find it easy to relax and express my feelings freely.	2	1	0
I recognize early, and prepare for, events or situations likely to be stressful for me.	2	1	0
I have close friends, relatives, or other people I can talk to about personal matters and call on for help when needed.	2	1	0
I participate in group activities, such as church and community organizations, or hobbies that I enjoy.	2	1	0
Stress control score: ___			
Safety			
I wear a seat belt while riding in a car.	2	1	0
I avoid driving while under the influence of alcohol and other drugs.	2	1	0
I obey traffic rules and the speed limit while driving.	2	1	0
I am careful when using potentially harmful products or substances, such as chemicals, poisons, and electrical devices.	2	1	0
I use a cell phone and/or I text while driving.	2	1	0
Safety score: ___			

Scoring key:

Scores of 9 and 10

Excellent! Your answers indicate that you are aware of your health and are practicing good health habits. As long as you continue to do so, you will not run into any serious health issues.

Scores of 6 to 8

Your health practices are good, but there's room for improvement. Look at the items you answered with *sometimes* or *almost never* and see what changes you can make to improve your score. Even a small change can help you achieve better health.

Scores of 3 to 5

Your health risks are showing! You need to learn about the risks you're facing and about why it's important for you to makes changes in your behaviors.

Scores of 0 to 2

Obviously, you were concerned enough to take the quiz, but your answers show that you're taking unnecessary and serious risks with your health. Maybe you're unaware of the risks and what to do about them so go to the student health center and seek counseling as soon as possible before your health gets worse.

Diets that Fight Illness

Just as certain foods – those high in saturated fat and simple sugars, for example – make us more susceptible to illness and disease, many foods make us feel energized, mentally alert, and keep us resistant to disease. For students, it's important to boost energy levels and maintain good mental health. The following are a few health and nutritional tips that will keep the mind-body connection working at full capacity.

- **Eat well-balanced meals.** Students are notorious for not eating right and not getting the nutrients they need to perform well in school. Since breakfast sets the stage for the rest of your day, never skip a good, nutritious breakfast of protein and complex carbs. Avoid sugary cereals, doughnuts, and bagels unless they are 100% whole wheat.

Include fiber, which lower cholesterol, stabilizes blood sugar, and rids the body of toxins.

- **Include foods that boost immunity**. Stress depresses the immune system, lowers resistance, and makes you more prone to all kinds of illnesses and diseases. Students often get sick not only because they don't eat well but because they eat foods that cause illness rather than fight it. To prevent getting sick, eat plenty of fruits and vegetables, fish such as salmon and tuna, whole grains, and nuts such as almonds and walnuts.

- **Count your calories**. The number of total calories you need depends on your age, weight, gender, and how active you are. Not getting enough calories will make you feel fatigued and slow down your metabolism. Just as gasoline fuels a car engine, calories from food is the fuel that gives you the energy you need for daily activities. On average, if you're not active, you need to be eating between 2000 and 2500 calories per day. If you're active, you'll need more.

- **Be smart about snacking**. Despite what you may have heard, snacking is not always bad, as long as you snack on something healthy. If food is fuel, snacks are the additives. The best ones are high in energy like bananas, dried fruits, nuts, low-fat yogurt (without fruit on the bottom, which is mostly sugar), fig bars, grapes, strawberries, oranges, and whole grain cereals.

- **Don't ignore minerals**. The only part of your diet that isn't created by a living organism is minerals, which you need even more than the vitamins that get all the attention. Minerals are what make enzymes work efficiently, they help build cells, and they maintain and revitalize organ systems. By consuming proper amounts of minerals, especially when stress robs you of those minerals, your body will repair and heal itself naturally.

- **Give supplements a try**. Though you should be getting your nutrients from the foods you eat, sometimes it's impossible. That's where supplements come in. Naturally you can't take every supplement that you see advertised in a health magazine, but there are a few that are more important than others. They are:

Multivitamins: Since most students don't think about eating a well-balanced diet, they may need a daily multivitamin as an insurance policy. Get a good name brand that also includes minerals. For best effects, split the vitamin and take one half in the morning and the other half at night.

Vitamin D: Whether you're a student or not, new research has shown that this is the most important vitamin that anyone can take in that it prevents more diseases than any other supplement. The majority of people are Vitamin D deficient, so the recommended dose is 1000 IU per day. Many doctors are now urging people to take as much as 2000 IU a day of vitamin D3.

Fish oil: Omega-3 fatty acids, found in cold water fish such as salmon and tuna, are essential because your body doesn't make them. They reduce the risk of heart disease, reduce inflammation, and play a crucial role in brain function such as memory and performance. The best fish oil pills are ones that contain a 3:2 ratio of EPA and DHA, the two main fatty acids. If the label on the bottle does not indicate EPA and DHA, don't buy it!

Probiotics: These are foods like yogurt that contain high amounts of beneficial bacteria, which are needed for proper digestion and strong immune function. Avoid yogurts with a lot of sugar, and opt instead for low-fat Greek yogurt, which contains twice as much protein and calcium as most other yogurts. Yogurts with fruit at the bottom may taste good but are usually high in sugar. As an alternative, you can buy easy-to-use capsules such as OrthoMolecular Ortho Biotic and take one a day.

Exercise and Health

Throughout the book, I've emphasized how important exercise is to reduce stress, cope with burnout, help you concentrate and study, and keep you physically and mental well. However, you may find that you're so busy with school and other activities that you just can't fit in a regular exercise program. If that's the case, there are many other ways to keep fit and healthy without having to go to the gym every day. Here are some tips for those too busy for regular trips to the gym:

- **Walk or take your bike to school.** If you live on campus or close by, walk to school or ride your bike instead of driving or taking the bus.

- **Register for physical fitness classes.** As long as you have to take a certain number of PE courses for your major, why not choose the ones that will give you a workout?

- **Take the stairs.** I'm always surprised when I see students taking the elevator to go up one or two floors. My rule is to never use an elevator unless you have to climb at least five flights. If you do that for all your classes, you'll get in shape quickly.

- **Take a hike.** Most campuses have large grassy areas and hiking trails. Spend some of your time just walking around and enjoying yourself.

Of course the best way to stay fit and make sure you're getting enough exercise is to maintain a regular exercise program. It's even better if you follow the suggestions above, as well as go to the gym for a scheduled workout. If you do, the following tips will help you prevent injuries and make sure you get the best workout you can.

- **Always stretch and warm up.** Before you do any kind of exercise, spend five minutes stretching and warming up your muscles. If you're going to lift weights, get on a stationary bike and peddle for five minutes before stretching. This warms up your body and prevents strains.

- **For cardio, do HIIT.** Most students don't have the time to spend 60 minutes on a treadmill. Besides, it's unnecessary. HIIT or high intensity interval training is the most efficient and productive type of aerobic training. 15 minutes of HIIT is better than 60 minutes of slow and steady cardio. Here's a typical HIIT workout on a stationary bicycle (you can do this on a treadmill as well):

First 3 minutes: warm up peddling

Next 60 seconds: peddle as fast as you can

Next 2 minutes: slow peddling

Next 60 minutes: peddle as fast as you can

Next 2 minutes: slow peddling

Next 60 minutes: peddle as fast as you can

Next 2 minutes: slow peddling to warm down

Next 60 minutes: peddle as fast as you can

Final 2 minutes: slow peddling to warm down

The beauty of HIIT is that your metabolism will remain high for at least 24 hours as compared to one hour with normal cardio. That means you'll be burning calories for an entire day. The other advantage is that you'll be out of the gym in a quarter of the time.

- **When lifting weights, do compound exercises.** The best exercises are ones in which you use multiple joints. These are the big four: squats, bench press, overhead press, and deadlifts. Isolation exercises like bicep curls and leg raises work a single joint and are not as effective. So to be as efficient as possible, drop the curls and do compound lifts.

- **Use free weights whenever you can.** Exercise machines are good and have their place, but the problem with machines is that they restrict you to a certain motion. Free weights force you to use the small accessory muscles that don't get developed when using machines. This can result in injuries because the larger muscles get stronger while the supporting muscles stay weak. That's why you can't lift as much weight when using dumbbells and barbells as you can when using machines.

- **Change up your workout from time to time.** If you stay with the same workout for more than a few months, your body will adapt and eventually not respond. Surprise your body periodically by changing the exercises you do, the number of reps you perform for each exercise, or the order of exercises. Regardless of what you do, confusing the body causes it respond by burning fat and building muscle.

- **Use the proper supplements.** Exercising, especially weight training, breaks down muscle fibers and uses a lot of energy. To make your workouts more effective, you need to help your body recover. Timing your supplement use is also important. Some supplements have to be taken at certain times to maximize your workouts. Here are the rules:

First thing in the morning: As part of your breakfast, make yourself a whey protein drink. The whey protein gets into your system very quickly, replenishes the proteins lost during the night, and keeps you feeling full longer.

Before a workout: 30 minutes or so before you work out, eat a protein bar and a piece of fruit for energy.

After a workout: Within 30 minutes of finishing a workout, drink a whey protein shake (about 20g of protein) and eat some healthy carbs like a banana.

Before going to bed: Instead of eating an unhealthy snack before bed, drink a tall glass of milk or a casein protein shake. The casein is a very slow digesting protein and will get you through the night without your body breaking down muscle. Never eat foods loaded with sugar before going to bed because they spike your insulin and suppress growth hormone.

Herbs and Your Health

If you're stressed or are getting sick more often than usual, you might be tempted to supplement your normal diet with herbal supplements. Other students may tell you that an herb is very helpful when in fact just the opposite is true. Besides, everyone is unique, and how one person reacts to an herbal supplement may be totally different to how someone else reacts to the same supplement. So be very careful when a fellow student suggests that you take a certain herb.

Some herbs are very beneficial; others are useless and even dangerous. A few may interact with any medicines you're taking and cause serious side effects. The following lists include the most and the least beneficial herbal supplements:

Most beneficial herbal supplements

Cayenne: helps circulation by lowering blood pressure and LDL.

Chamomile: helps relax and aids sleep.

Cinnamon: lowers cholesterol and helps regulates blood sugar, which prevents insulin spikes.

Fenugreek: helps lower cholesterol and may help control blood sugar levels.

Garlic: improves the cardiovascular system by helping lower blood pressure, LDL, and triglycerides.

Ginseng: controls blood sugar levels and helps in healing.

Oregano: has antibacterial properties and helps with digestive, skin, and respiratory problems.

Rosemary: rich in antioxidants, it may protect cells against cancer and radical damage.

Turmeric: a powerful anti-inflammatory and antioxidant, it helps prevent joint pain and may prevent tumor formation.

Valerian: relaxes muscles and helps sleep.

Least beneficial herbal supplements

Aristolochia: may cause kidney problems and cancer of the urinary tract.

Borage Seed Oil: may cause stomach disorders and/or liver damage.

Calamus: may cause dizziness, nausea, and hallucinations.

Cat's Claw: may cause diarrhea and hypotension.

Chaparral: may cause liver failure.

Coltsfoot: may cause tumors and liver cancer.

Comfrey: may cause cirrhosis and liver failure.

Echinacea: may cause upset stomach, diarrhea, constipation and dizziness.

Ephedra: linked to at least 100 deaths due to cardiac arrest and stroke.

Eucalyptus: may cause skin problems, convulsions, and seizures.

Foxglove: may cause nausea, vomiting and, in some cases, cardiac arrest.

Germander: may cause hepatitis, chest pain, and breathing problems.

Kava: may cause fatigue and liver damage.

Lobelia: may cause nausea, vomiting, diarrhea, and rapid heart rate.

Pennyroyal: may cause nerve damage, convulsions, and seizures.

Pokeweed: may cause nausea, vomiting, diarrhea, and rapid heart rate.

Sassafras: may cause hallucinations, high blood pressure, increased heart rate, muscle spasms, and paralysis.

St. John's Wort: may interact with other medications; may also cause dizziness, headaches, confusion, and GI disturbances..

Yohimbe: may cause renal failure, seizures, anxiety, panic attacks, stomach disorders, paralysis, and cardiac arrest.

The Importance of Sleep

We all know what it's like to go without enough sleep. We can't concentrate, we become irritable and moody, we get mentally fatigued, and we're more prone to illness and disease. So there's no question that sleep is critical for good physical and mental health. As a student, sleep is especially important because you need to be alert and stay focused, not only during class but afterwards while you're studying.

Students also need to maintain a regular sleep schedule so that they maintain a proper biological clock. The worst thing you can do is sleep a full eight hours one night and then four the next, or go to bed at 10 PM on Monday and 3 AM on Tuesday. All you're doing is continually resetting your body's natural cycle and falling into a pattern that leads to insomnia. The following are some suggestions that will break your disruptive nighttime habits and make you feel more energized.

- **Avoid caffeine before bed.** Coffee is a big culprit in keeping you awake, but other products contain caffeine also. Soft drinks, chocolate, and tea may not contain as much, but they contain enough to keep you awake. Products like energy drinks often have two or three times the caffeine as coffee, so avoid these altogether, especially at night.

- **Keep your room dark.** Even a light from the alarm clock next to your bed may cause a change in brain melatonin and disrupt sleep. So, turn off the TV, shut the blinds, and turn the alarm clock around so that your room is completely dark.

- **Avoid alcohol at night.** Although alcohol is a central nervous system depressant, it causes you to wake up several hours later and makes it harder to fall back asleep. When you do fall asleep, your sleep won't be as restful as it would have been without alcohol. Besides, don't condition yourself to depend on anything to help you fall asleep.

- **Go to bed at the same time each night.** The worst thing you can do to disrupt your body's natural biological clock is to be constantly resetting it. If you go to bed at different times each night, your body simply can't adjust and will resist attempts at forcing it into an unnatural schedule. The best way to get into a good sleep habit is to develop a routine so that you can transition easily from day to night..

- **Wake up at the same time each morning.** If you sleep in late on the weekends, your internal clock will naturally readjust itself by Sunday evening. So even if you stay up late on weekends, you need to force yourself not to sleep more than an extra hour or so before getting up. Staying in bed until the afternoon just one day will set you up for days of poor sleep.

- **Don't exercise late in the evening.** Exercise increases blood circulation to the brain, which keeps you alert and awake. It also triggers release of adrenaline, the hormone responsible for increasing heart rate and blood pressure. The best times to exercise are morning, afternoon, or at least three or four hours before going to bed.

- **Avoid stimulating activities before bedtime.** Don't assume that using your mind will tire you out and make you sleep better. Just the opposite is true. Your brain becomes over-stimulated and you end up thinking too many thoughts, which keep you awake. Your body needs to know when it's time for sleep, so clear your mind of distractions, and never do homework in bed. Watching an action movie or reading a thriller in bed keeps you stimulated. Instead, wind down with something that's not so exciting.

- **Use relaxation techniques.** Relaxation exercises have a natural tranquilizing effect that can induce sleep. Use the techniques in the previous chapter to trigger a deeply relaxed state and help you fall asleep more easily.

- **Watch what you eat before going to bed.** The rule is to not eat a heavy meal, especially one with lots of carbohydrates, three hours before going to bed. The increased blood circulation caused by digestion will interfere with sleep. If you need to eat something before bed, choose protein instead. A glass of milk is also a good option because the tryptophan in milk, which is converted to serotonin, induces sleep.

You don't realize how important sleep is until you start having sleep problems. By then it's going to affect your study habits and your learning and make you much less productive. Because the physical effects of sleep deprivation add up over time, you're also going to become less resistant to illness and disease. By getting a good night's sleep every night, you'll not only feel more refreshed and energized, you'll stay much healthier as well.

Premenstrual Syndrome (PMS)

Affecting nearly ninety percent of young women at some time in their lives, PMS is usually linked to periodic hormonal changes, especially estrogen cycles. PMS can also be triggered by changes in brain chemicals before menstruation, or by stress and/or social factors. If you suffer from premenstrual syndrome, don't ignore it since PMS can seriously interfere with concentration, learning, studying, and test-taking, all of which will affect your grades.

Symptoms of PMS may last a few days to as many as two weeks and include depression, anger, irritability, fatigue, water retention, anxiety, and emotional problems. If you find yourself suffering with PMS, there are some effective strategies that work well. They are:

- **Decrease saturated fats.** Going to fast food restaurants and eating hamburgers and fries is one of the worst things you can do for your health in general. If you have PMS, saturated fats only add to the problem. So eat plenty of fish, fruits, vegetables, beans, and high-fiber whole wheat grains and cereals.

- **Eliminate water to reduce water retention.** If you experience water retention and bloating before or during your menstrual cycle, decrease your water intake. Also, decrease your salt intake as well, since salt causes you to retain water.

- **Eliminate simple sugars.** Avoid foods that have a lot of sugar and empty calories. That includes doughnuts, soda, junk foods you get from vending machines, white bread, and sugary breakfast cereals. Simple sugars spike your insulin levels, make you crash, and cause your symptoms to become more severe. If you crave sugar before and during your menstrual cycle, try supplementing with 500 mg of magnesium, which helps reduce the cravings.

- **Take a multivitamin with minerals.** Because of their hectic lifestyles, most students don't get the proper amounts of vitamins and minerals, so take a multivitamin each day.

- **Exercise regularly.** Not only does regular exercise help manage weight, stabilize hormones, and keep your heart and bones strong, the endorphins that you released during exercise reduces stress, lifts your mood, and keeps you emotionally balanced.

- **Get enough calcium.** Studies show that you can significantly reduce mood swings and cramps by taking 1000 mg of calcium daily.

- **Avoid caffeine, tobacco, and alcohol.** All of these can make your symptoms worse. Avoiding them will also help you sleep better, which lessens PMS symptoms.

Seasonal Affective Disorder (SAD)

Some individuals become depressed or moody during the fall and winter months because of insufficient light exposure. This happens more commonly in northern areas where winter days are typically very short and there's a big difference in the amount of sunlight between seasons. SAD is basically a change in your biological clock, when daily biological rhythms get out-of-sync with the sun. Your brain's chemistry is altered, and you begin to feel depressed.

Like other types of depression, SAD can be genetic and it tends to run in families. It's also three times as prevalent in women. Symptoms can vary, but the most common are sadness, withdrawal, fatigue, sluggishness, increased sleep, moodiness, irritability, and the inability to concentrate. These can be mild or severe depending on the individual. So how do you know if you have SAD or if it's something else? The following are the four clues that doctors use to diagnose SAD:

1. For at least the past two years, you feel sad and depressed during the fall and winter but are back to normal during the spring and summer months. Symptoms come and go about the same time each year.

2. When fall arrives, you begin to crave carbohydrates like bread and pasta, and you start to gain weight.

3. You sleep more than usual during the fall and winter.

4. You have a close relative with SAD.

For students, SAD can be devastating and debilitating because it interferes with study schedules and the ability to study, do homework, and learn. Don't ignore the warning signs, especially if they're impacting school life. If you think you're suffering with SAD, here are some things you can do:

- **Increase social activities.** A vicious cycle begins to develop as winter blues take over your life. You do less and you become moody and depressed, which then makes you want to do even less. To break the cycle, plan regular events with friends. Just getting out more and interacting with others will get you into a better frame of mind.

- **Increase outdoor physical activity.** In the winter, people do winter things like bowling, going to movies, or staying home and watching TV. Instead, take walks, take a ride, enjoy the fresh air. Make it a habit to spend several hours a day outside. The less active you are, and the more time you spend indoors, the worse the symptoms will become.

- **Alter your diet.** The worst dietary culprit during winter is too many simple carbohydrates. Instead of pretzels or potato chips, both of which are full of empty calories, eat fruit, raw veggies, and more proteins.

- **Change your indoor environment.** How you live has a profound effect on how you think and feel. The simple act of moving furniture around and placing couches and chairs near windows, where you'll be exposed to more light, can make a big difference. Also helpful is opening blinds to allow as much sunlight in for as long as possible, increasing wattage of light throughout the house, and repainting walls a light color to reflect incoming sunlight.

- **Use light therapy.** If all else fails, there are several types of light treatment. One of them is bright light therapy, which involves sitting in front of a special light box that's much brighter than normal indoor illumination for at least 30 minutes a day. Another option is called dawn simulation, which mimics the increasing light of morning. A special dim light comes on early in the morning and gets brighter, just like you were waking up to sunrise. You can purchase either of these from online merchants such as Amazon.

- **See your doctor.** If nothing else is working, and your symptoms are causing severe problems, pay a visit to your doctor. He/she may prescribe a medication that will stabilize brain chemicals and get you back into a normal rhythm. Another option is melatonin supplements, which some studies have shown can be very effective in treating SAD.

10 Final Student Health Tips

The following are 10 final health tips that students can use to make school healthier and more enjoyable.

1. **Avoid all-nighters.** Cramming until into the night is going to drain your energy, impair your ability to learn, and decrease your immunity and resistance, which makes you even more prone to illnesses. It's much better to study all along and get a good night's sleep every night.

2. **Quit smoking.** This one's a no-brainer. Smoking causes a rash of illnesses and diseases, including lung cancer, emphysema, and hypertension. So if you smoke, quit; if you don't smoke, don't even think about starting. The health center at your school should be able to offer the help you need.

3. **Drink in moderation.** Students like to party and have a good time, but drinking excessively leads to weight gain, hangovers, inability to focus on school work, and increased health risks. If you're going to drink, do so in moderation.

4. **Get regular checkups.** Just because you're in school doesn't mean that you should ignore regular exams. Everyone should be getting an annual checkup; and if you're a woman, schedule breast exams and pap smears during breaks.

5. **Get your flu shot.** The flu can be severe enough to land you in bed for days and will cause you to miss valuable class and study time. To avoid a disruption to your school work, make sure you go to the health center and get vaccinated.

6. **Drink enough water.** Dehydration causes a host of health problems, including high cholesterol, high blood pressure, and blood sugar. In addition, it can interfere with focus and concentration and make learning that much more difficult. Drinking enough water will also keep you from overeating and help you stay away from junk food. An added benefit is that it will flush harmful toxins out of your body.

7. **Don't skip meals.** Skipping meals is one of the worst things you can do for your metabolism. By not eating regularly, your body goes into a defensive mode and stores fat because it thinks you're starving it. So to keep on an even keel, eat every three hours. Three healthy meals and two healthy snacks in between is the perfect way to stay healthy.

8. **Avoid foods that cause fatigue.** Foods high in sugar give you a quick energy boost, but it's short-lived. Within an hour or so, the energy boost is followed by a crash because you've spiked your insulin levels. To keep your sugar levels constant, choose foods that are high in fiber. The 5 worst foods for triggering fatigue are white rice, white bread, soda and other sweet drinks, fast foods, and sugary snack foods.

9. **Wash your hands.** There are a lot of germs going around campus, particularly during the winter months, so wash your hands often, especially when you're in contact with a number of other students and especially during cold and flu season.

10. **Set realistic goals.** Realize that you can't do it all and maintain healthy stress levels. Being realistic about what you can and can't do will help you maintain emotional balance and well-being.

Be proactive about your health. No one can keep you healthy as well as you can. So be your own health guru. Be aware of any changes in your health, don't avoid seeing a doctor if you feel you need to, and don't allow others to tell you how to live your life if you know that it will cause health problems. Be assertive and say no to that extra drink or those extra fries.

Between the lectures, exams, study sessions, sports activities, and social events, students have a lot going on. So it's not surprising that so many students end up getting sick. Your physical and mental health should be a top priority, not only because it will make you feel better but because it will make you a better student and result in better grades. By following the suggestions in this chapter, you should remain healthy and disease free.

Index

ABOUT THE AUTHOR

Dr. Andrew Goliszek is an Associate Professor of Biology at North Carolina A&T State University in Greensboro, NC. For more than 25 years, he has taught courses in Biology, Anatomy & Physiology, Zoology, Endocrinology, Animal Physiology, and Mammalogy. He has also been the recipient of several NIH grants, has written numerous books and articles, and is winner of the prestigious Outstanding Teacher of the Year Award.

www.ingramcontent.com/pod-product-compliance
Lightning Source LLC
LaVergne TN
LVHW051522080426
835509LV00017B/2162

9780615568126